NORA TRIMS HER LAMP

an autobiography

Nora Ruiz Ednacot Brozo, BScN, RN

Nora Trims Her Lamp
Copyright © 2017 by Nora Ruiz Ednacot Brozo, BScN, RN

No part of this publication may be reproduced, distributed, or transmitted in any form or by any means, including photocopying, recording, or other electronic or mechanical methods, without the prior written permission of the author, except in the case of brief quotations embodied in critical reviews and certain other non-commercial uses permitted by copyright law.

Tellwell Talent
www.tellwell.ca

ISBN
978-1-77302-447-9 (Hardcover)
978-1-77302-446-2 (Paperback)
978-1-77302-445-5 (eBook)

This book is lovingly dedicated
to the memory of my dear son,
Brian Thomas Brozo.

"Till we meet again at Jesus' feet."

ACKNOWLEDGMENTS

Above and foremost is my profound gratitude to the Most High God for His divine intervention in writing this book. I stand humbled at my Master's feet, ever grateful for His pruning of my life and for His boundless grace which allows me to work in His vineyard.

My heartfelt thanks to Pastor Efenito Adap for the one-on-one Bible study he gave me in 2002 that led me to experience the saving grace of Jesus and my total submission to the call of Baptism as a Seventh-day Adventist Christian.

To Pastor Ben-Ezra Adap, for patiently reading and editing my manuscripts, giving direction and serving as my adviser, and helping my young faith be more grounded upon a theological standpoint.

To Pastor Dr. Nerval Myrie, my baptismal officiating pastor; Mrs Olga Lawrence; and Sherry Grossett; my enormous gratitude to you will never be sufficient, and in no way could I reciprocate your encouraging words. You offered prayers after prayers in the hours of my deepest sorrow and despair over the cries of my innermost heart. In my most troubled and saddest moments, your listening ears on the phone day or night surely settled the fall of my teardrops.

Now is my opportunity to thank all of my family, relatives and friends, along with Brian's former schoolmates and classmates who in one way or another stood by him from the beginning of his ordeal to his very final moment.

I salute all of Brian's dedicated friends: Mark, OJ, Irena, Neil, Jacque, Andrea, Puya, Kevin, Rene, Habib, Ralph, and Jonathan and very many others. If I missed your name, I solicit your forgiveness. With just a moment's notice you would show up at Brian's bedside. Brian's friends took time off, finished work early, and came, rain or shine. These were their unselfish gestures just to be able to be with their friend Brian. And I am ever so moved looking back to a time when five or six of these loving friends decided to turn their car around and head back to Toronto. They let go of their long planned trip because of a suffering friend in need. Talk about the amount of tears they shed on Brian's parting. Together you gave such an unbelievable love, sincerity, and loyalty that I have since treasured in my heart.

To Kuya Rem Brozo, I am so moved just thinking about you. You and your ever loving late Susie wonderfully supported your late nephew in a multitude of ways. Our late Ate Susie is sadly no more, but she was one amazing woman. She too is definitely in the hearts of many.

To Brian's godparents Ate Charit and Kuya Rolly, you never failed to visit Brian at home or in the hospital throughout those ten solid years. I must have thanked you before but it is worth thanking you again.

To Mareng Eppie, Pareng Rudy, Mareng Cora, and Pareng Cris, my heartiest thank you. You stood by me literally and unselfishly on very many long nights to console my grieving and bleeding heart. Your love and kindness have always been in my heart's treasure box.

To Glendor Miller, a grand thank you my dear friend for being there when no one else was, even when you were dead tired. Glen, you are one of the best indeed. None other but you believed and personally encouraged me in this book and my radio broadcastings. You even got up early one morning just to listen to my very first radio streaming in the Philippines on "Jesus, My Lord Jesus is Everything", or "Jesus, ang Panginoon Kong si Jesus ay Lahat-Lahat".

To Dexter, Cathy, and Christine, this is what Mom has been up to. There was never a night that you and the little ones were not in my prayers before I lay my head to rest for the night. To my grandchildren Sydney and Max, someday you shall understand what Grandma has been called to do for our Lord Jesus. I love you so dearly and I am mighty proud of you both.

Last, but never least, I want to use this space to thank my husband and life partner, Tomas (Matt) Brozo for adding the spice to my life's story, without which I could not and would not have completed this volume.

To you, dear readers, it is my joy to sincerely invite you to journey with me through the next pages of this tiny and blessed book that is now in your hands. All in the mighty name of Christ Jesus, Amen.

PREFACE

The very God Who scatters abroad His immense wisdom is the very same God Who engineered and designed the entire universe, both animate and inanimate. Since time in eternity, He is the immutable God Who remains unchanged. His nature exhibits eternal love. Shrouded in mystery, He wisely planned His work and implements this work in righteousness. His transcendent nature makes Him unfathomable, His greatness immeasurable. Yet He is also an immanent God, Who being big makes the heavens His dwelling, yet He can dwell in the hearts of His created beings who lovingly submit to Him.

Out of His great love, He wanted to impart the knowledge of Him and find someone to communicate His will. He wanted His love be known to all who - like Him - choose to dwell together in harmony and in loving kindness.

This very God spoke through His prophet Isaiah to declare His blessed intention, and Isaiah obediently wrote:

7 Everyone who is called by my name, whom I have created for my glory, I have formed him, yes, I have made him. 8 Bring out the blind people who have eyes, and the deaf who have ears. 9 Let all the nations be gathered together, and let the people be assembled. Who among them can declare this, and show us former things? Let them bring out their witnesses that they may be justified; Or let them hear and say, "It is truth." 10 You are my witnesses says the Lord, and my servant whom I have chosen, that you may know and believe me, and understand that I am He; before me there was no God formed, nor shall there be after me. 11 I, even I, am the Lord, and besides Me there is no other. 12 I have declared and saved. I have proclaimed and there was no foreign god among you; therefore, you are my witnesses, says the Lord, that I Am God. (Isaiah 43:7-12).

Ever since I have come to personally accept and know my God, I have pledged to be one of His humble witnesses, and to testify He is my God and that there is no other comparable to Him. He has proven to me that He can work wonders with the great and even with the small. My humble life's story is one example of how My God found me.

It took some forty years, not because God was slow as many would think and surmise, but because I was seeking Him in the wrong places. Yet God mysteriously worked wonders behind the scenes of my life and called me in His own good time. He has proven again in my tattered experience that His word is true and can be trusted. He can transform lives; make the insignificant, significant; and the immaterial, relevant and useful. I am inviting you to walk with me along the trail that I have walked. Together, let us smell the fragrance of flowers, feel the cooling showers, and from this thorn- and thistle-strewn pathway, may you discover God, His love, and His peace.

May we experience His invigorating presence and His healing power, and may we allow Him to restore our broken relationship with Him. Learn with me as I relate my eventual escape from the abyss of spiritual darkness into the exciting kingdom of light.

Nora Ruiz Ednacot Brozo, BScN, RN

INTRODUCTION

It has been said and quoted so many times that "every story has a beginning." This book is no exception, for since the time I was born, my life began telling the many beginnings of ever changing vistas, portraying countless colourful experiences in my tattered life existence. Many of those occurrences were filled with challenges that are common to many people, then and now: to wives and husbands, mothers and fathers, and men and women in general.

This volume portrays my life's pilgrimage through roads of ups and downs, along the trails of flowers and thorns, cheered by sunshine and challenged by alarming rains, until I came to the crossroads of my life. The choices I have taken may be helpful to anyone who arrives at these crossroads. My choices did not instantly usher me toward a life of affluence, nor did they provide me with a bed of roses. Instead, the choices I made helped me define my life's destiny with an assurance of a joy that lasts forever. The journey I took changed me as a person, ever since I discovered a spiritual relationship with One Supreme Being - God, Who can turn defeat into victory and Who can make the common, significant.

My life has taught me much about human subsistence. Some were hard lessons to learn, some were pleasantly woven into my lifestyle, while other significant pieces of wisdom minted me amidst tears and agony. There were times when I found my life standing alone in the crossroads of life, confused and not knowing what I needed to do until that Someone extended His help and patiently guided me to the right path I needed to take.

Therefore, let me share my life's testimony whose sentiment relates to the tenor and lyrics of this gospel song below: ***At the Crossroads,*** *written by Alberta M. Paris.*

Nora Ruiz Ednacot Brozo

How often we stand at the crossroads of life,
Bewildered, dismayed and alone;
No marker to guide us thro' tempest and strife,
The highway unnamed and unknown.

No sound in the silence, no friend standing by,
No star in the darkness of night;
But still reassuringly rings the old cry:
"Lo, I am the Way and the Light."

One road may lead down a deep valley of doubt,
And one may wind over the hill,
But Jesus, with hands reaching tenderly out,
Is waiting and loving us still.

(Refrain):

But Jesus is there at the crossroads,
Unguided no more you need roam;
His strength will provide you,
His wisdom will guide you
To the way of the cross leading home.

MY HUMBLE BEGINNING

The Creator of the universe meticulously and wonderfully knitted me for nine months in my mother's womb until my schedule arrival on December 12, 1952. My birth coincided with the historic swearing into office of the newly-elected president, Elpidio Quirino, the second president of the Independent Republic of the Philippines, succeeding former President Manuel Roxas.

My coming to this world was during a time of restoration and healing of the nation. The whole country was still reeling from the ravages of World War II, and the young republic was quelling the agitation of the resurging post-war guerrilla in Luzon, who were conniving with the communists. This element was fast becoming the new menace to the nation's peace and stability. The rebels were commonly known as Huks, a short name for *Hukbong Bayan Laban sa Hapon,* which means People's Army Against the Japanese. Whatever semblance of peace the nation enjoyed could only be traced among the quiet, lowly citizens working to find their way to normalcy, healing, and recovery. Whether this period surrounding my birth would have an influence on the life and profession I would choose, only the great Designer of the universe knows.

My father Ernesto Ednacot, who hailed from the island of San Salvador, married Francisca Segundo Ruiz, one of the daughters of Alejandro and Januaria Ruiz. I am sixth of the seven children of Ernesto Ednacot and Francisca Segundo Ruiz, and I am fourth among the daughters of my loving parents. I was raised by this peace-loving family nestled in a small island of San Salvador, an island guarding the Masinloc Bay, a rural territory belonging to the municipality of Masinloc, which holds the distinction of being the first town organized in the province of Zambales in 1607.

There are other smaller isles surrounding San Salvador and one of those isles is named Magalawa, a small islet owned by Alejandro Ruiz and spouse Januaria Segundo Ruiz. Planted with coconut, the isle of Magalawa produced copra (dried coconut meat), a coconut product that commanded a good price in the market. They had their premium property duly registered in the Office of the Registry of Deeds in the province of Zambales in 1923.

The owners of Magalawa Island, Alejandro Ruiz and spouse Januaria Segundo Ruiz, subdivided the property to their children according to common family tradition during those times. For a time, in the life of Masinloc, the Ruiz clan reaped high regards of the town folks, with some even named to public office. For years, *copra*, the prime product of their island property, was marketed by our grandmother to Chinese businessmen in Manila for a sizable sum of money.

San Salvador was formerly known as Salvia Island when the Spanish explorer, Juan de Salcedo, discovered it in 1572 and named it. It has a land area of 230 hectares and is divided into four political sections called *sitios*. Looking at the traces of the once beautiful Island of San Salvador, I could only say that it could have been much more beautiful had it not been adulterated by people who do not know the God of creation. Youths from the island sought the high roads of education, found employment outside of the island, and even travelled abroad. Now San Salvador dwellers are trying to preserve the footprints of the Almighty, that it would not be erased completely nor altogether be obliterated by adding man-made places of amusement. Gone are the smooth white beaches and the crystal clear sea water lapping the immaculate shore. Just as what happened to God's beautiful Eden paradise after sin had greatly changed it, so is San Salvador now. The evil of this old world could not spare this once beautiful little island paradise.

People living in these islands thrive mainly on fishing or farming. My father supported our family by working hard on his decent piece of land and supplementing his income through some fishing when farming season was over. The piece of land was more than enough to produce and sustain the family's basic needs, and my wise father made provisions for the future wellbeing of his family.

My father was a proactive forward thinking farmer. He made some simple investments in preparation for the health, education, and growing needs of his seven children. He assigned a section of his land for orchards, which he planted with different fruit bearing trees. I believe he must have planted these trees years before I was born, for I remember all of them bearing delicious and luscious fruits during fruit-bearing season such as guavas, *atis, tisa, guyabano, sinigwelas*, papayas, and coconut trees. We had one huge *sampaloc or tamarind* tree that provided our house with good shelter and a cool breeze.

My growing years were never boring. As a child I found excitement chasing our chickens around. The stillness and serene atmosphere of the neighbourhood was broken only by barking dogs, early morning crowing of the roosters, and squeaking piglets as they impatiently waited for their herders to feed them. We also had one carabao, my father's most treasured livestock. Carabaos are swamp-like domestic water buffalo which provide the necessary labour that allow Filipinos to grow rice and other staples. These beasts of burden provided my father with all the help he needed during farming season, as well as in hauling and transporting our farm products. Mechanized farming had not yet entered the minds of the Filipinos during those years, especially not among the dwellers of San Salvador.

Some hundred yards from the house was the fish pond that my father and relatives had designed. In this pond, my father farm-raised *bangus* and other fresh water fish. My sister Linda and I used to have fun as we dipped ourselves in the pond and experienced the fish tickling and even nibbling on our toes. My father set up a manmade trap called *"hiklong"* to trap and catch the edible crustaceans living in holes beneath the mangroves. He also had a pretty large fishing net, called a *"palakaya"*, which he commonly used when fishing in shallow waters.

The portion of the sea separating the island from the mainland was deep and of a frightening dark-blue colour. I dreaded imagining our loaded *banca* (dugout canoe) capsizing. When our *banca* was loaded with the many farm products to be sold to the market, just one careless move would be enough to tip one side of the boat and then we would be gone. But we always had the reassuring eyes of our father upon us as he paddled the boat with ease. I watched the bulging muscles of his chiselled physical frame while his strong arms guided the boat towards mainland Masinloc and back to the island. Nevertheless, the sight of the beautiful corals deviated my fear of deep waters.

Evenings in our home were filled with interesting pastimes. A kerosene-fuelled lantern, as our main mode of lighting, illuminated all our family activities in the living room. Some would study school assignments and complete homework, others along with my mother would play *sungka*: a game played on a solid wooden block with two rows of seven circular holes and two large holes at both ends called the head. This game is also played in other Asian countries like Indonesia and Malaysia, where it is known as *congkak*.

It is common among the houses in the island of San Salvador to have only one or two bedrooms, and a living room serving as the common bedroom for the children. At bedtime my eldest sister would usually spread open the *banig* (a large mat made from woven buri leaves) on the bare floor and we younger ones would determine our respective sleeping spots. My brothers would unroll one large *banig* for themselves on the other side of the living room. When my father extinguished the kerosene lamp, that would signify it was time for quiet and sleep.

Planting and harvest times were exciting in my native land. To the farmers, the planting season was a season of hope. They would toil hard and sacrifice sweat and blood. My father used to invite young couples to help him during the planting season. He would make the fields plant-ready, and on the scheduled day the invited young couples would come to help. Thus, the planting would be completed by the end of the day. This cultural practice of the Filipinos is called *bayanihan* (literally meaning heroism) where a group of villagers would come to help a member of the village finish an important task. In most cases, when starting or finishing a job that called for many hands, the owner would organize a *bayanihan*. This act of the neighbourhood would be reciprocated through the privilege of being invited back during the harvest and given a fair share. Harvest season was festive and filled with revelry. The sweet aroma of *pinipig* was a welcome delight. *Pinipig* is a Pilipino delicacy of roasted freshly harvested grain. When it is pounded and the husks are removed, it serves as a satisfying delicacy.

During the *bayuhan* (rice pounding festival), the rhythmic sound of pounding rice served also as a dancing beat for itchy feet with an inclination toward dancing.

Memories of my father are revelatory for me. I never saw him attend church, but he was godly in his manners. He loved my mother like a fragile and expensive vessel. His love for my mother and to us his children were his signature of how caring a man he was. He taught us children virtues of self sacrifice and frugality in every gift that comes from God. Who else could have given my father such wisdom, but the Holy Spirit that comes from God? Godly virtues come from God. The word of God says, *"If you then being evil know how to give good gifts unto your children, how much more shall your Father in heaven give the Holy Spirit to them that ask him?"* (Luke 11:13)

MY PREPARATIONS FOR LIFE

Beginning with my grandparents and down through the generations, my family were strong believers in education. My folks were determined that their children be given the best education possible. My parents knew that the pursuit of education would be daunting, and would ultimately entail a pure determination of the will between parents and children. They hoped that their children, upon reaching the age of accountability, would display a readiness to learn and be educated.

My generous grandparents who situated their dwellings in the Magalawa Island were concerned for the wellbeing of their children and their families who were living in San Salvador Island. My grandfather's generous heart thought of putting his money toward the best welfare of his children. There were times when the sea was rough and dangerous for a small sea craft to be flying the waters morning and afternoon while loaded with little school children and farm products. My older siblings Berting, Flora, Virginia and Cesar would many times voice their growing fear of a dangerous sea crossing on a fragile sea craft. This matter was not left unheard by our generous and very caring grandparents. They responded to these concerns by having a house built in the town proper of Masinloc for their daughter Francisca and her whole family.

The location of the house my grandfather built was a great relief for my parents and to us children in our pursuit of education. My grandfather also helped my mother to finance a small *Sari-sari* (variety) store that augmented the family resources. That was the beginning of our eventual assimilation to urban life from the island of San Salvador to the town proper of Masinloc.

Being the youngest among four girls, my mother endearingly called me little *Noying (Nora-Darling)*. A mother's instinct makes her overly protective of the fruit of her womb. At a very young age I contracted a peculiar illness called juvenile rheumatoid arthritis, also known as juvenile idiopathic arthritis. According to doctors this is the most common type of arthritis in children under the age of sixteen. Juvenile rheumatoid arthritis causes persistent joint pain, swelling, and stiffness. Some children may experience symptoms for only a few months, while others may have symptoms for the rest of their lives. The sporadic and severe pain in both of my legs resulted in sleepless nights. I couldn't play with the other children in the neighbourhood and I had difficulty walking to and from school. At the young age of seven, my mom had to carry me on her back to school. She would come back at the end of the school day to collect me and give me a lift back home. The two-and-a-half kilometre walk could take my mom almost an hour with me on her back. She needed to put me down several times along the way to rest her back. She religiously offered me a piggyback ride to school every day for several weeks until my leg pains subsided and I eventually overcame my physical handicap. Subsequently, my older sister Linda was tasked with looking after me on our way to school, in case I needed her help.

The generosity of my grandparents and the convenience of town living made our schooling hassle free. The property in San Salvador was still being managed by my father. On top of this, he had begun mapping the plan for my secondary education.

My high school education began at Northern Zambales Academy, an academy catering to the educational needs of the youth in Masinloc. It was here that I was introduced to higher education and my physical and mental development was greatly enhanced.

Early in high school, my womanhood started to show, and somehow this caused the heads of some boys to turn. Like a budding rose, I was fast becoming the cynosure among the boisterous male population in the school campus. Older folks talked, though maybe not seriously, and my mother warned that certain parents had insinuated their liking that I would be their daughter-in-law. However, rather than allow these accolades of my dainty demure looks to take root in my head, I just quietly concentrated on my studies.

But, it was then that a man from our town, a fresh biochemistry graduate from University of Santo Tomas, Manila, got me scared. He belonged to an affluent and respectable family, and he was eight years older than I was. At that time, high school girls were very particular about age gaps when considering who to be paired with. But this mestizo guy was different. From the first time he saw me, he gave me long, lingering looks that scared me. My parents were aware of how insistent this man was in pursuing me. Before my lengthy walks from our house to school, I was always reminded by my mother to be extra careful. The fear of being abducted was slowly taking root inside me. This scenario continued through my first three years of high school. He used all his connections to try and get me to at least speak to him, but my parents and I were on the same page that I did not want to entertain this man in any way. He was completely obsessed with me, but I kept eluding and avoiding him. Perhaps I was too young and naïve about falling into a relationship.

My sister Flora and her husband Froilan arrived from Hawaii to reside in the city of Olongapo while Froilan, a U.S. Navy Officer, was stationed at the Subic Naval Base. They convinced me to stay with them so I could be of help in looking after their three-year-old son. My parents did not think twice about this arrangement, and I was told off you go, Nora. And so I finished my fourth year of high school at St Joseph Catholic High School in Olongapo City. I thought I would finally be relieved from the pestering of my ardent suitor, but somehow he obtained my address and his love letters came one after another.

When I started my preparatory nursing course in Manila, I learned that the man who was so crazy about me had left to go and work in the United States of America. Once again, he came to know my new address and continued to pursue me through his very eloquent letters. Not a week went by that I didn't receive one or two letters from him and all sorts of cards that carried messages of his honest intentions and love for me. His letter writing did not stop there, for this person came to also know my telephone number, and so both his letters and his overseas calls became commonplace. I only spoke on the phone to him briefly, as this was my first overseas call and I was very nervous. I didn't reply to his letters, although I was beginning to feel guilty for receiving them. During my first year of internship at the Chinese General School of Nursing I finally replied to one of his very many letters. I simply acknowledged that I had received his letters and cards, and then I told him to take care.

This mysterious person then sent me a short note expressing his profound thanks and joy, for "the ice, finally, was broken." Our friendship started to bloom from a distance. He became my boyfriend and I became his girlfriend through letters.

My parents did not need to encourage me to become a nurse, for in my young student days I was fast developing a love for adventure. I was already one of the many young girls obsessed with going abroad and seeking adventure in the land of opportunity, the land of milk and honey so they say - Canada, America, Australia, or anywhere outside the Philippines where the way of living and pay are better. The nursing profession was the fastest at hiring for positions abroad, even many years before I graduated.

NURSING PROFESSION BY HEART

While studying my two-year preparatory nursing courses at Far Eastern University in Manila, my grasp and knowledge of the nursing course began taking a new turn. It was at this learning institution that I came to learn about the birth of the nursing profession and how it was professionalized by a certain woman named Florence Nightingale. Nowadays she is an icon of the nursing profession. Her life story fascinated me and created a deeper impact upon me as I read from the book, *The Lady with a Lamp*. I considered her a heroine who had made the noble contribution of self-sacrifice and love for the nursing profession.

Florence Nightingale is widely known in all schools and colleges of nursing worldwide. I was greatly emboldened by her belief and strong desire to devote her life to the service of others, for she had been prompted and called by God. She was nicknamed the Lady with a Lamp during the Crimean War in 1855 in reference to her compassionate walking back and forth through corridors in camps and barracks to comfort the sick, dying, and wounded soldiers of the war when all of the medical officers had gone to bed for the night. Florence, alone with her little lamp, walked along the long halls and corridors, from one room to another, to provide comfort and aid to the wounded and dying soldiers of the war.

After my graduation from the Chinese General Hospital School of Nursing in March, 1974, I pursued my degree in nursing at the Manila Central University through supplemental schooling. It is only through the grace of God that I succeeded through all of my schooling years. I was just an average student who had learned not to give up, no matter what. I was a persistent and persevering student. I could not afford to disappoint my parents who I dearly obeyed and loved. My early impression of nursing was of plain academics, and I needed to find a better job placement. I was like a lamp without oil, until I began to understand the depths, heights, and widths of the nursing call.

I stand privileged and blessed by the Father for the wonderful profession that He permitted me to have for a good forty-two years. The experience that I have had in this arena of caregiving were enormous and profound.

Nursing is filled with endless personal rewards and fulfillment. It is a profession that never stops the art of giving. Everyday you will touch a life and somehow, in some degree, a life will touch yours. By making a difference in the lives of others, there is unexplained joy and contentment with a humbling and tangible results no amount of money can buy. Nursing is never just a job or a mere profession. It's a high calling that involves inseparable elements of love, compassion, kindness, gentleness, dignity, courage, endurance, humility, self-sacrifice, and many more attributes; there are too many to enumerate them all. Nursing is not just about giving pills, administering intravenous antibiotics, monitoring inotropes, measuring cardiac outputs, monitoring ventilators, emptying colostomy bags and other drainage bags, preventing skin breakdown, managing bedpans, providing wound attention and care and countless other nursing measures - there are way too many responsibilities to describe them all. Nursing does not only get into your skin, but it is absorbed through you and becomes all of you. It has been said that it takes your whole body - all senses, your mind, and your spirit - to empower you to execute what you have been called for: to care for the well, the ailing, the recovering, and the dying.

There are numerous frustrations in nursing coupled with challenges. Though you express your desire to make a difference, some will dislike you. But you will be consoled by those who believe in you and bless you.

In nursing, you will see life begin and end. You will see people at their best and at their worst. Many nurses have also learned to close their eyes and bite their tongue after having been abused physically or verbally by however manner and degree. And worst of all, nurses are subjected to psychological abuse: "I want my medications now"; "I do not like you, get me another nurse"; and "I will report you". And yet nurses must carry on and finish their shift no matter how much humiliation they receive. You may find some considerate and compassionate doctors who acknowledge that you work like a dog most of the time from work overload. Then again, there are times you will have to bite your tongue for their rude and harsh words that a taskmaster would say to a slave. Yet a nurse by heart will hug a patient to show sympathy and assurance. A nurse will sometimes forego the call of nature in favour of the patient's needs, because a nurse believes this to be his or her calling.

As a nurse I found joy from announcing the triumphant arrival of a newborn baby. I shared the joy of new parents upon the good tidings heralding the arrival of a bouncing baby boy or an adorable baby girl. There are moments too when, with teary eyes, a nurse must say with a heavy heart, "I am very sorry, but she did not make it. You have lost your loved one, dear."

To be a nurse can never be an accident - it is a prerogative. You must choose to do what you can when others can't and won't. Commonly we hear, "I could never do what you are doing; I do not know how you do it." But thanks be to God, nurses exist as angels of mercy, attending with compassion twenty-four hours a day, seven days a week, winter, spring, summer, and fall, never breaking the continuity of care from the very moment a patient lies down on that hospital stretcher or bed.

Nurses are in fact peculiar but wonderful vehicles of heaven. Of the innumerable patients in the course of one's career, each and every one comes seeking care and help. They are all the same people whom Christ, the Messiah, has sought, bled, and died for.

The nursing profession is far more than the rendering of optimum physical care, for most of all, when an illness has gone irreversible, and when patients have turned from bad to worse, and they have reached their point of deepest need, nurses have the divine opportunity to offer what you may be longing for, the intervention of a higher being that no medical management can equate - God.

In times like these, a prayer offered petitioning that the God of heaven will pass not the tears of the sorrowing families often serves as a balm to soothe pain and anguish. Offers of prayer are highly received, appreciated, and very seldom rejected. A nurse is a picture of multiple ministries in most instances. Her presence alone is already a gesture of compassion and care. Her tender touch of a patient's hand serves and infuses assurance of companionship. Her ability to listen to complaints is another; hence, when prayer is offered, most patients willingly submit and appreciate. The intimate pleadings and ardent prayers of His children are never ignored by our ever compassionate and loving heavenly Father.

I cannot help but utter my profound thankfulness to God as I reminisce on my development as a nurse, a tool of care and mercy in His hand.

I cared for an imminently dying child from a debilitating disease. This was my first time shedding tears at a bedside as I watched her Cheyne-Stokes breathing that I had first come to learn as a student nurse. The mottling and ever cold skin and bone and pretty much motionless limbs were tightly held by the mother, who was begging God for last minute help, not to allow her little one to release the last breath. Even when the final hour had come when God's precious little one had to be pronounced lifeless by the doctor, the agonizing mother just couldn't let her baby go. The scenario gave me several sleepless nights.

My practical nursing experience had instilled in me the nature and extent of my chosen vocation. I must be willing to spend my life caring for those who were in dire need of caring hands and a shoulder to cry on. Would I measure up to the challenge? I mused.

Graduation day came and my parents were so proud of me, like any parent who sees the fruits of their labour and objectives reached. Out of the seven children in the family, I was their second nursing school graduate. But several months before graduation I had met the man I was destined to spend the rest of my life with: Tomas Brozo, *Tom* to friends and *Matt* to his immediate family, a fresh Electrical Engineering graduate of Mapua Institute of Technology in Manila. He was present during my graduation and it was upon my introduction that my parents knew and understood that my "single status" had changed. The call of love made me transgress my promise to serve my parents for at least two years or even for a short period of time. I knew they were disappointed and greatly disheartened.

TOMAS (TOM/MATT) BROZO

My last year of clinical nursing at the Chinese General Hospital was an unforgettable chapter in my life's chronicles.

At the medical surgical floor where I was assigned came an admission of fifteen-year-old Romy Centeno, a vehicular accident patient from the emergency room. On arrival, Romy's face was badly swollen, and there were bruises around his eyes and on different parts of his limbs. He had also sustained fractures on his legs, and we were warned that he had sustained some brain concussion from the accident. Romy arrived with his very frightened family and several friends.

To us student nurses, Romy's case was a fairly interesting one for our clinical studies, as he was a patient with both orthopedic and neurologic issues. I braced myself for the new challenge. For days, Romy was not able to recognize his family. He was ever restless and had slurred speech. He had episodes of nausea and vomiting every now and then, which were relieved by anti-emetics. His mother and sisters took turns staying with Romy twenty-four hours a day. The whole family was very kind and always grateful for every little care that Romy received from the nurses.

Romy showed remarkable improvements during the following weeks and proved to be one amicable and friendly guy. He was surrounded by faithful friends and loving relatives during his stay at CGH, all of them wishing and praying for his quick recovery. It did not take longer than a month for the doctor to give Romy a discharge order.

Romy's full neurologic recovery was amazing. I knew he had been supported and prayed for by many. The family promised a thanksgiving party upon Romy's discharge, and I was one of the several nurses invited. I never imagined the remarkable event that would unfold in my life upon attending Romy's party.

At the thanksgiving party, most of the attendees were male with a sparse number of ladies from the school of nursing. As was common in those days during gatherings of eligible ladies and gentlemen, matchmaking would take place through teasing and pairing games as long as the party lasted. But my situation was different, for at that time I already had a biochemist boyfriend in the United States. We had maintained good communication and we would not betray our relationship. So I distanced myself from the fray of teasing and matchmaking. Isolated from the group, I discovered a waiting chessboard with all pieces rightly positioned. I kept wondering who could have prepared the chessboard, and I was expecting a chess enthusiast to suddenly appear and play. Yet I saw that no guest was venturing to play except myself. With nothing to do, I amused myself with some chess moves and tactics while quietly sipping a bottle of soft drink. Behind the kitchen curtain, a tanned young man was keenly watching every chess move I made and stealing a glance at me every now and then. On most of those instances our eyes would accidentally meet. His looks and stare were not empty, but emphatic and enchanting. Before I knew it, he came closer to ask whether I knew how to play chess.

"Yes," was my unscripted reply.

"Can I play with you?" He shyly added in a humble tone, "I am still learning, and I just want to hone my chess moves."

"So," I said to myself, "I am going to beat this man."

Over the course of the long game that followed he inquired about the visiting hours in the dormitory. Between moves the meaningful stares were becoming longer. And though I won the game, I realized that he had allowed me to win, for I later learned that he was one of the best chess players of Mapua Tech. He introduced himself as Engineer Tomas (Tom/Matt) Brozo, an electrical engineering graduate of the Mapua Institute of Technology (MIT). I discovered and learned in our ensuing conversation that he was then working at Subic Naval Base in Olongapo City. From this initial acquaintance, this young engineering graduate had unsuspectingly drawn me into a tactical game just like the game of chess we had played. Was I in for a checkmate? The cupids must have been smiling.

I was very surprised when Matt did visit me at the dormitory the following weekend. That visit was followed by another visit and still another. I tried to avoid him during his early visits, for I did not wish to betray my boyfriend who was in the States. I would go swimming at the YWCA at Buendia just to avoid him and go back to the dorm when I thought all visitors had gone, but Tomas Brozo was still there and wouldn't leave until he saw me. By then I had received a letter from my boyfriend in the United States heralding the news of his homecoming.

In December 1973, my boyfriend arrived and insisted that we be married that same month so that he could take me to United States of America. If I wouldn't do this, then it would be the end of our relationship. I never felt any urgency nor excitement from his offer. I broke up with him, for I could not imagine the thought of missing my forthcoming graduation in March, 1974, and putting to waste the sacrifices made by my parents. They were looking forward to my graduation which by then was only three months away.

Unknowingly, I made the noble decision of completing my education. I didn't know that the wise man Solomon had counselled this so long ago: *"Choose my instruction rather than silver; and knowledge, over pure gold. For wisdom is far more valuable than rubies. Nothing you desire can be compared with it. Wisdom, live together with good judgment..." (Proverbs 8:10-12 NLT)*.

I could not believe I had found enough courage to choose graduation in place of a marriage proposal and hurried wedding with my long-time boyfriend. His selfish ultimatum proved to me that he was not the man to whom I would devote my affection. I never missed my boyfriend when he left in a huff for America, nor did I feel a loss of someone dear to my heart.

I was oblivious that my life at this point could be likened to a game of chess. I had made a move that appeared to be a good winning move, not knowing that my playmate was orchestrating a move to his advantage and would win the game at all costs. His was a stronger and more advantageous move. My move of breaking up with my boyfriend of two years became an opening for Matt to advance his agenda. Matt saw a potential ending of the game. He was winning. Check after check ensued. I surveyed my remaining pieces on the board. I had spent them all and beheld not a bad resignation but a glimmer of hope for both of us.

During one of Matt's frequent visits he said to me: "I see in your face that you will be the mother of my children." (Check!) I understood he was not jesting. Although he always spiced our conversation with humour, his voice carried a solemn message of responsibility. I remember blushing while trying to find out whether Matt was talking to someone else. But I saw his eyes fixed on my very own pimple-sprayed face. He was talking to Miss Nora Ruiz Ednacot, the young energetic lady who had blossomed into a compassionate and caring nurse. Now, I was seeing this funny guy, so caring and loving and serious in expressing his intentions. "Was he for real?" I thought to myself. His visits were timely, and he showered me with beautiful flowers and apples. He introduced me to his family, so I knew that he was sincere in his intentions. My attraction to him blossomed into an affection I had never felt before. I came to realize that I loved him. (Checkmate?)

Passionate love is very strong. It can transcend beyond borders and despises all else just to follow her plaintive call. My love for Matt was strong. My attraction for this naturally curly-haired guy grew together with the growing locks of his hair. My respect for this dark skinned young man kept increasing as he fulfilled his work responsibilities, never retreating from the heat of the burning sun. Likewise, my love for him mounted every passing day. My young electrical engineer loved his job at the Subic naval base in Olongapo City. In return, his job loved him too. A wise man said, "Love your work and your work will love you." It's a saying so simple and yet so profound.

MARRIAGE AND FAMILY LIFE

"Place me like a seal over your heart,
Or like a seal on your arm.
For love is as strong as death,
and its jealousy is as enduring as the grave.
Love flashes like fire, the brightest kind of flame.
Many waters cannot quench love,
neither can rivers drown it.
If a man tried to buy love with everything he owned,
his offer would be utterly despised."

(Songs of Solomon 8:6,7 NLT)

My parents never disputed my relationship and ultimate decision to marry the man who had become the apple of my eye, even after a very short courtship of one year. I knew too that my parents lovingly prayed for their new son, Matt, to whom they entrusted the future of their daughter. They handed me over to Matt, trusting that Matt would love and cherish their special darling daughter the way they had loved and protected her. They were praying, I believe, that Matt would treasure me the way they had first treasured their vibrant, talkative, and friendly little *Noying* twenty-two years earlier. The sanctuary of the University of Santo Tomas Church, bedecked and made ready for the occasion, welcomed the two contracting parties of the Ednacots and the Brozos, to witness the union of two lives under the blessings of matrimony. The guests inside the adorned sanctuary of the University of Santo Tomas Church were all smiles on that day of October 19, 1975. Assured greetings and congratulations reverberated from wall to wall. Yet, outside the church, a storm was raging and flooding the city thoroughfares. The well-pressed trousers of the groom were dripping wet when he arrived. The organist was absent due to heavy rains. There was no instrumentalist to play music. The church organ was destined to remain quiet until the service was over. The traffic had become very slow due to the areas that had been flooded. Motor vehicles became stranded and pedestrians sought more passable routes.

The wedding ceremony, nevertheless, proceeded as scheduled. In the conspicuous absence of the church organ music, the officiating minister and my man, Tom, occupied the side of the altar as the signal for the wedding processions to begin. Even without the pompous love tunes of the bridal march, I thought I looked my prettiest in my simple bridal gown. I saw Matt at his handsomest in his *Filipino Barong* outfit. As my father walked me down the aisle to give me away, my mother's eyes met mine. Her eyes were filled with tears, as were the eyes of other mothers present. Why were people weeping, when this day was a day of celebration and gladness, when two hearts were joined together as one? Well, whether Mom knew the Holy Scripture or not, it is true that *"Unless the Lord builds the house, the work of the builders is useless" (Psalm 127:1, NLT)*.

Through experience and acquired wisdom, the old folks knew the perils brought by ill-prepared marriages. Parents have witnessed couples in constant antagonism ending in divorce and separation. Some homes endure the pain of indifference and violent animosities lurking within the walls. How many couples knew and heeded the holy counsels of the Lord regarding husbands and wives? Regarding wives, the Bible says, *"You wives will submit to your husbands, as you do to the*

Lord. 23For a husband is the head of his wife as Christ is the head of his body, the church; he gave his life, to be her saviour" (Ephesians 5:22-23, NLT).

And how equally solemn is the counsel for husbands: *"25And you husbands must love your wives with the same love Christ showed the church. He gave up his life for her 26to make her holy and clean, washed by baptism of God's word. He did this to present her to himself as a glorious 27church without a spot or wrinkle or any other blemish, instead, she will be holy and without fault. 28In the same way, husbands ought to love their wives as they love their own bodies. For a man is actually loving himself when he loves his wife" (Eph. 5:25-28 NLT).*

Parents are aware of the many unions that were only after the fantasy of emotional and physical excitement, while denying the deeper substance and spiritual essence of marriage. How many couples considered this before contracting marriage? How many young couples understood that marriage goes far beyond the physical feelings? I admit, I was not prepared nor well-equipped to face the spiritual spectrum of marriage. Couples need to understand that marriage is not a competition between two heads, straining the veins of their necks while trying to prove who is in the right and who is in the wrong. Marriage is a life of being together as one: *"A man shall leave his father and his mother and be joined to his wife, and the two become one flesh. Whatever therefore God has joined together let not man put asunder."*

Marriage is a team with each member happily supporting and working for the welfare of the other, and not of one member alone. Marriage is living together and finding life together, because the two have been made one.

I saw the sadness in my parents' faces the day I marched down the aisle with Tomas Brozo. Was it because my parents wanted me to linger with them for a while, helping the family? Were those tears caused by disappointment that they had not seen their daughter don her immaculate uniform through two years of loving service to a rural community, as was mandated for nursing graduates by the government at that time?

Since the first day Matt had been introduced to me by Romy, our friendship had grown so fast. In the matter of a year, we had tied the *proverbial knot* to love and cherish one another as long as life shall last. We were both wishing and praying that the proclamation by the officiating minister would come true, that *"what God has joined together shall not man separate."* I was utterly enamoured and felt like I was floating on cloud nine, believing everything was heavenly until we entered into the marriage chamber and enjoyed the sacred pleasures of two hearts joined as one flesh. Every passing day became a learning episode for both of us, as a young couple.

Matt and I lived for some time at Don Quixote, Sampaloc, Manila, in one simple room as our first little nest as husband and wife. Matt's work contract at Subic Naval base in Olongapo was cut short to give preference to our would be growing family.

It was providential that my sister Virgie's sponsorship which she filed for me before my nursing graduation was accepted and at the same time our application as immigrants to Australia was also approved. Nevertheless, the Lord paved the way that we come to join my sister Virgie and her family in Hamilton, Ontario, Canada. While working for our Canadian visa, our first child announced his coming. Dexter, our firstborn child, first saw the light exactly nine months after our marriage. Dexter's arrival was a great blessing in strengthening the bond of love between me and my husband. Our waiting for the long awaited travel visa was appeased by the energy and antics of our first son, and my love for Matt grew sweeter as the days went by.

In September 1977 with two moderate suitcases, fly now pay later plane tickets, a few dollars in our wallet, and our miserable teething ten-month-old Dexter we boarded the plane. Our send-off by two huge families made us appear like movie stars.

Oh, Canada! Our (destined) home and adopted land. We were so elated to safely land as new immigrants of Canada, a land "glorious and free." Through my sister Virgie's generosity, our adaptation to Canadian life was made smooth and pleasant. Matt was immediately blessed with a job as an electrical maintenance staff of Glendale Spinning Mills in Hamilton. After less than a year of staying with my sister and her family, we were able to move to a two-bedroom apartment of our own a few days after the arrival of another precious jewel, Brian Thomas.

For our basic apartment needs we started out with hand-me-downs, courtesy of my ever generous sister Virgie, newly met friends, the Salvation Army, and garage sales. We used a loaned crib for the new baby. But for several weeks the three of us slept on the floor until one day Matt gave me the best news and I jumped for joy. It was like winning in the lottery when he said he was approved for a small bank loan, enough for that cheap bedroom suite that we had prayed for. God's grace after grace came, and I babysat one beautiful little Italian girl for two dollars per day. It did help with buying groceries. Matt learned to trim his own hair and mine, as we were extra careful to our very last penny.

MY RELIGIOUS ORIENTATION

From elementary school, to high school, to university, I was a regular Sunday church goer and very devout Catholic. I considered myself super religious. I was religious in the sense that I had never violated church protocols as prescribed by the Catholic church and according to my interpretation of them. However, religiosity is not necessarily spirituality. I religiously attended mass every Sunday, but from childhood until I turned forty, I did not know the spiritual significance of the Eucharist that was being celebrated. Unaware, my life was sinking deeper in a dark alley of spiritual ignorance. I was made to believe that my faithful church attendance and good deeds would ultimately be reciprocated with salvation, which would land me in heaven. Yet I had no knowledge whatsoever about the Bible, God's Holy Book. All the while I had believed that my salvation would depend largely on how I made myself holy in every task. I didn't know that the Bible's teachings were quite contrary to my belief. For it says, *"For by grace you have been saved through faith, and that is not of yourselves, it is a gift of God. Not of good works lest anyone should boast"* (Eph. 2:8,9). This Bible verse proclaims that good works have no part whatsoever in salvation, and that no one should boast of his or her religiousness and good deeds. So, where have my good works gone? What about the many who believed as I used to? I felt like I was trapped in a suffocating darkness. Like one who has been trapped in darkness, I began my search for the light of a truth I had never known. The mysterious unfolding of light that came to me became the compelling theme of this volume.

A glimmer of hope beckoned me. I need not be deceived and misled. Before, I would return home from church assuming that I had been made holy by my Sunday mass attendance and participation. Like many others, during church services I would roll my rosary beads, never attentive even to short sermons of the priest. Sometimes I even practiced kneel-walking. I would do my own thing while mass was in progress, or while others performed the so-called stations of the cross. During the mass, my eyes would focus on the statue of the supposed saint for whom the church was named after, for I was there to ask for something that would somehow lift my extra pressing burden, like passing my exams. Frequently I would make requests, ask for favours, or repeatedly pray to God, whom I did not know.

I would turn to the statues for favours. And whenever favourable events occurred, I would presume them to be requests granted, though I did not know which one of the images had granted my requests, whether it was the patron saint or God Himself. I was ignorant as to how I could develop and establish an experiential relationship with the deity they called God. I had never consciously acknowledged that it is a personal relationship with God that matters most in life, no more and no less. Like many Catholics, I was one of many who had never received a thorough indoctrination of God and Jesus Christ, and so I had blindly assumed that I was a good Christian, when in fact I was lost in the darkness of ignorance.

The popular Quiapo Church was one of my favourite churches to go to. At Quiapo church, I could do *kneel-walking* (walking on bare knees) to profess my pressing need for help, especially before examination days. Many claim that a lot of miracles occurred in that church because of the image of the Nazarene that sat there. I was among the many who carried a handkerchief to wipe the feet of the image of the Nazarene, believing that the handkerchief would become miraculously blessed, capable of wiping off illnesses and discomforts. All the days of my youth I had blindly participated in this heathen practice, a practice which ultimately brought me to hopelessness rather than the confidence and assurance of a Christ-centred life.

At one point I heard about a Christian ministry called the "Lord's Flock." The group was conducting meetings at the square downtown. I located the meeting place and discovered that their speaker that day was a woman. They introduced themselves as honest seekers, but I did not understand what they were seeking. Anyways, I had the opportunity to be there and observe their lively interactions. The lady speaker spoke with confidence, testifying that God's blessings come *"well pressed down, shaken and overflowing"*, alluding her message to Luke 6:38 of the gospel. I was very impressed by her confidence and knowledge in speaking about God, and by the end of the occasion I said to myself, "I would like to be like her one day, Lord. I could also make people see and know you." But my assumption was meaningless. If only I had known what Jesus lovingly reminded His disciples: *"I am the vine, you are the branches. He who abides in Me, and I in Him, bears much fruit; for without Me you can do nothing"* (John 15:5).

The Apostle counseled thus, *"In your relationships with one another, have the same mindset as Christ Jesus: Who being in very nature, God, (He) did not consider equality with God something to use to His own advantage; rather, He made Himself nothing by taking the very nature of a servant, being made in human likeness"* (Philippians 2:5-7 NIV).

I was still blind and insensitive to the initial working of the Holy Spirit in waking up my soul from slumber. But unknown to me, by God's providence the Lord had placed a certain lady in my life who I secretly admired. Almost daily, I quietly observed her strange behaviour and noticed her uniqueness. Her lifestyle caught my attention.

I had nine roommates in the dormitory of the Chinese General Hospital School of Nursing. One lady named Sally Distajo was a professing Seventh-day Adventist Christian. She was the only Adventist among the 1974 class of graduating nurses. She caught my attention in various ways. Sally was one peculiar saint in her simple manners of speaking, dressing, and eating. I found her time and again on her knees with bowed head to say her prayers each night after reading her Bible. She never missed reading her Bible before she went to sleep, while we, her roommates, would roll our own rosary beads only on some nights. There were days when we teased Sally about her Bible reading; we even warned her that she might overshoot heaven due to her devoutness. Sally must have felt sorry for us, because she would volunteer to pray for us on our behalf. In spite of her gentle and gracious manner, I had the temerity not to ask her. I would say that this lady bothered me, not in a negative sense of the word, but I was bothered by her kindness and spirituality. Sally was not practicing her devotion because of wanting to be saved or her desire to go to heaven. Instead, I learned she was doing this because, as she said, *"when she was yet a sinner and lost, Christ died for her sins."*

It was a new puzzle that had never before registered in my thoughts. She was keeping a constant communication with her Forever Friend, Jesus. Slowly I felt a hunger and thirst after righteousness. I could have thanked Sally for her silent testimony allowing us, her roommates, to read the gospel in her life. This could have been the unfolding of something significant toward my greatest discovery. In His boundless love, God was patiently working on me.

ENCOUNTER WITH A SPIRITUAL GIANT

I had a face-to-face encounter with a national figure, one famous International Preacher-Evangelist who has preached the Gospel in 185 countries and territories over six continents. Billy Graham Jr., an American evangelist and former spiritual adviser of American presidents, was admitted at MICU of Toronto East General Hospital in June, 1995 after collapsing in front of a huge crowd of 62,000 people during his crusade at Toronto's Skydome.

I was probably the most curious nurse of the unit wanting to personally see this world-renowned preacher. Mr. Graham was under the care of our cardiologist, Dr. Bentley-Taylor. During his stay in the hospital, adjacent rooms were deemed "No Admission" for security reasons and his rooms were well-guarded from inside and out.

Denise, one of the most senior nurses, was assigned to be his attending nurse. I repeatedly offered my help should she need any, for we all knew that Mr. Graham was one overly tall person. And the time came that Mr. Graham had to use the commode chair. As Denise and I were in the motion of getting him up, words just came out of my mouth, unplanned. I said very calmly, "Pastor, do you mind if I say a prayer for you before you get up?" And of course Mr. Graham was surprised. The guard in the room was also surprised, as was Denise, in hearing this suggestion came from a tiny nurse who was trying to be of help.

And Mr. Graham said, "Oh thank you," and he bowed his head. We all bowed our heads, and I said:

"Father, please heal your servant from the top of his head to the soles of his feet." Then I said, "That is all, Pastor."

And he said, "Thank you; I certainly needed that."

And we carried on proving the care that Mr. Graham needed at the time. As I stepped out of the room I said to myself, "My God, I prayed over the world-renowned preacher face-to-face, and it was the shortest and the most intimate prayer of all prayers." I had forgotten the fact that this man of God is also a man of prayer himself. Perhaps the number of prayers he has prayed would compare to the prayers of a saint. Yet he was so humble and submissive to the prayer of a little nurse with a man-sized faith. The Bible says a lot regarding prayers:

"Likewise the Spirit also helps in our weaknesses. For we do not know what we should pray for as we ought, but the Spirit Himself makes intercession for us with groaning which cannot be uttered" (Romans 8:26).

Yes, regardless of our status, we all need God's help. We all need prayer, and we praise God for the experience. The ministry of prayer proves to be helpful clinically and emotionally. We ought to pray always.

MY GREAT DISCOVERIES

I had thought I was very religious. I learned early in my young age how to correctly make the sign of the cross and would even teach my mother every time she got confused about how it was properly done. I often went alone to our church in the town of Masinloc. Although there were no church services, I simply sat silently in one of the pews and talked to any of the images around me, regardless of their identity.

I did not know who most of them were. I remember the countless times when I would speak to one crucified image, wondering who he was, and why he was hanging on the cross. I remember the many times I stared at the image of the infant Jesus and wondered why this infant was included among the saints.

When I was about forty, I believed in the existence of God, but I still had no clue as to who God really is. I was still ignorant. Had this God any claim on me, and what relationship did I have with this God? What had I to do with Him? I wondered how many were in this same condition, and like myself, prayed and paid homage to statues and images who couldn't hear nor feel why they needed my worship and adoration.

While my second son Brian was fighting a fierce battle against lymphoma, I was also battling spiritual ignorance. My thirst for truth became so intense. I thirsted to find God and discover Who He is. I realized I was sinking in the depths of helplessness and badly needed help.

My meeting with Carmen Dimaapi was providential and the doing of God. My new friend offered to study the Bible with me, and invited me to join her. I readily consented. She introduced me to Pastor Efenito Adap and his wife at the house where the Bible study was in progress. They sang, *"God is so good, He's so good to me."* I mused and thought that God indeed was so good for opening an opportunity for me to grow in my knowledge of Him.

My friend sat beside me to guide me in locating the Bible verses. I noticed that Carmen had no difficulty in finding the Bible verses which proved and answered every question relating to our subject of discussion. I also noticed that her Bible had been carefully marked and well indexed by her. I felt embarrassed when I saw Carmen's Bible. If someone like her still felt the need to study the Bible, I should too, for I felt I needed to know a world of knowledge relating to God's love for me and for all mankind. I felt humbled and my religious ego began to crumble. A new spiritual struggle raged within me. I was still holding onto my own old wineskin of religious orientation.

The unrelenting love and mercy of God consistently nurtured my spiritual hunger. God's mercy followed me relentlessly and silently. Even while at work, He safely guided me. On one occasion, while I was looking after my ventilated patient in the MICCU of Toronto East General Hospital, Derick the Respiratory Technician came to check on the ventilator. He was softly singing. I faintly heard the words of his song and I asked him to repeat his song. Then, without further ado, he sang:

> *"In the morning when I rise,*
> *In the morning when I rise,*
> *In the morning when I rise,*
> *Give me Jesus.*
> *Refrain:*
> *Give me Jesus, give me Jesus,*
> *You may have all this world,*
> *But give me Jesus."*

What a nice song, I mused. So simply worded, yet it told a world of truth, of one willing to give up everything the world had to offer for Jesus.

Derick was his casual self, amicable and gentle in his manners, and one who would readily and confidently speak about his religion when asked. To my surprise his manner resembled that of Sally Distajo, my former classmate who was a Seventh-day Adventist Christian. This co-worker who worked as a Respiratory Technician demonstrated a calm spirit. He possessed a hidden reserve of kindness in his behaviour. I learned from him that he was also an Adventist Christian. Aside from being male, he reminded me of Sally Distajo, who was, like him, a member of the Seventh-day Adventist Church. Not to be intimidated, I bragged about my own Christianity. On one occasion my conversation with this co-worker touched upon the issue of salvation and getting into heaven. I pretended that I was in the light, while he was in darkness. I bragged about my religiosity, as a consistent Sunday keeper who seldom missed church mass, especially during holidays. I mentioned the fifty-two images of saints in my possession plus my expensive painting of supposed Christ. The statues that I collected for years were material objects, humans formed in male and female images out of stone, wood, cast metals, golden- and silver-coated metals, cement, and plasters attractively dressed and adorned with colourful outfits. I used to bow down before them for prayer and for help. I cried before them for my troubles and needs, lit candles, and offered beautiful flowers before them. But though they had eyes, they did not see; they had ears, but did not hear. They had feet but could not walk; they had mouths and lips but could not speak. Yet on that day I proudly mentioned how I revered each one of them. To my wonder and amazement, Derick did not challenge me; instead, he made the appealing offer: "Sister Nora, before you go to bed tonight please read 1 John 2:4." His suggestion was simple, and I felt I must follow it.

When I was getting ready for bed that night I remembered my co-worker's appeal to read the verse he had suggested:

"He who says, 'I know Him,' and does not keep His commandments is a liar, and the truth is not in him" (1John 2:4 NKJV).

I was blown away by the confronting message of the Lord. "What now, Nora?" I thought. This Bible verse bothered me for many days. During my attendance at the Bible Studies with Pastor Adap, I remember him emphasizing the role of obedience in the lives of the saved who love the Lord. For Jesus Himself said, *"If you love me, keep my commandments,"* (John 14:15 NKJV); then in chapter fifteen, Jesus illuminated it further, saying, *"If you keep my commandments, you abide in my love, just as I have kept my Father's commandments, and abide in His love"* (John 15:10).

Pastor Efenito gave further instruction on a one-to-one basis. The very enlightening and informative weekly Bible studies lasted for several weeks. The light of truth about God flooded my soul, as the story of salvation unfolded in such a simple manner that even a little child could understand.

If Jesus so loved the world, He so loved me too. If he died for everyone, then He died for me as well. And the big word "whosoever" qualified me also. Pastor Adap's prayer at the end of the series gave me sweet and tender assurance in Jesus. I went home with a song in my heart.

> *Blessed assurance, Jesus is mine,*
> *O, what a foretaste of glory divine*
> *Heir of salvation, purchase of God,*
> *Born of His Spirit, washed in His blood.*
> *This is my story, this is my song,*
> *Praising my Saviour, all the day long.*

While I was in solitude one evening, oblivious of my surroundings, the prince of darkness was close by, creating a battle out of his wrongs against the marching throng of right penetrating my soul. This inner warfare continued for some time. I found refuge and solace in my Bible studies at Carmen Dimaapi's house with Pastor and Mrs. Adap. I discovered that Carmen, although long in her faith, still felt that she needed her Bible. She had the sword of the Spirit and faith as her shield. My love for the Word of God grew and I longed to be close to my Lord. I was not aware that the prince of darkness was doing his cunnings by making my life miserable and hard. My son, Brian, was getting sicker each day. I had found a refuge now in Jesus and I wished I could impart that joy and hope to my son Brian as well as to my family. I felt jealous of Adventist people for possessing a serene spirit of security. If their serenity was because of their faith, then I must discover it. I began to long for that kind of faith possessed by people who have found refuge from life's care in Jesus, a kind of security in Jesus that changes burdens into blessings.

The Lord pieced together the missing fragments of my spiritual experience, though the enemy of my soul had subtly laid snares along my path. How cunning and subtle the devil was, in timing his snare to come when I was at the crossroads of a decision.

In the early part of January 2002, the Filipino Association of Mississauga had chosen me to represent Hermana Mayor for the year's festival of *Flores De Mayo* (Flowers of May Festival) that would coincide with the *Santa Cruzan de Mayo* (May Festival of the Cross). Every first week of May, Filipinos are fully engrossed by these events both at home and abroad. Other *Reynas* or Queens had been chosen, such as the little ones who would be attending the parade. They had already been named and informed as early as the middle of March. More than half of the preparations were completed, including the artificial flowers for the arks and the venue. The reception of more than five hundred Filipinos was already booked at the Mississauga Community Centre Hall. This highly awaited celebration by the Mississauga Filipino Association and its carefully charted schedule of activities would be followed religiously. To compound the challenge before me, I had a flight scheduled for Manila the week after the said festivals.

There are situations when God shows the wisdom of allowing man the freedom of choice.

I happened to find in the telephone directory the sign Mississauga Seventh-day Adventist Church, located at 2250 Credit Valley Road in Mississauga. Out of curiosity I said, "I have to visit that church," and I did. At that same time, during the early part of the year, I was already participating in the Bible study with Pastor Efenito Adap at Carmen's place. The missing pieces of my quest for peace were beginning to come together. Pastor Adap was very patient and accommodating of all my questionings. The way of the cross was leading me home.

It was due to God's scheduling that when I first entered the Mississauga SDA Church, that first Saturday of March, I experienced an awesome, inexplicable feeling of total surrender to God. I whispered a simple prayer and said, "Lord, the search is over."

The kind and friendly members ushered me in. The fellowship, singing, and interactions among the members were lively and authentic. I made a glancing survey of the well-lit sanctuary. It was so simple but orderly. There were no images.

All the people were happily greeting one another as if they were all a part of one big family. Some came to greet me and made me feel comfortable and at home. How different was the atmosphere of this church, different from the mystic services coupled with pageantry and monastic formalities of the church I had always attended for Sunday services. I had never before experienced any form of intellectual interactions but only dry fellowship. Sadly, I had been raised in the world's largest Christian church, where I, for forty years, had languished in complete spiritual darkness.

While in the pew, I began to feel like a lonely wanderer who had finally found her way home. I came to realize that there was no more need for me to search any further, nor to join any prayer groups of other denominational affiliations which had not meaningfully contributed towards my spiritual development and growth. My search for the church that stands in the platform of truth had finally come to an end. Now I had found the Christ of the Church. No more kneel walking, no more lengthy novenas, no more rolling of rosary beads. I was literally overwhelmed that the hands of God had finally led me to where I should be.

I found myself crying and weeping in the pew. I had finally come to an irrefutable conviction from my lessons and studies with Pastor Efenito Adap, when he had pointed me to the truth that "on the old rugged cross on the hill far away was Jesus, calling His children home."

Who were these people, composing the family of God on earth? My heart was filled with untold expectancy.

During my very first visit at the Mississauga SDA church, I did not know who Pastor Nerval Myrie was. Someone else introduced him to me as the Church Pastor. This pastor sat down next to me in the Bible study room. He watched me like I was one lost sheep, maybe because I looked lost in the group.

The questions coming from the group sounded very pertinent, and although I hardly asked any questions, Pastor Myrie gave me special attention.

On my second attendance to the church, I gleaned from the sermon of Pastor Myrie his exposition about the Searching God as he expounded on the kindness and mercy of God, the searching and finding God. I listened to him speak about this God, Who is patiently seeking and Who rejoices in finding, as He wants to establish a lasting relationship with His children. I found myself weeping heavily with indescribable joy. I was enveloped in a heavenly atmosphere I had never felt anytime or anywhere before. Right there and then I asked the Lord to search for me and find me.

I could not contain any longer my personal conviction, and so I literally told Pastor Myrie my longing to be baptized in the name of Christ, as soon as possible. My apprehension for the trip home to the Philippines would now be in the hands of God. I did not want to die without the Lord in the event of a plane crash, but there was something more beyond the reason why I needed to be baptized. I wanted assurance, should something happen during my travels. And by submitting myself to baptism, I wanted to profess and publicly declare my vow, that by faith, I was now a child of God. Right away as per God's own calendar we agreed that my baptism would be on the last Sabbath of the current month, my fourth Sabbath at the Church.

On that second week I formally withdrew my participation from the Festival of the Cross and ensuing Flores De Mayo where I was supposed to be the Hermana Mayor. My withdrawal from the Flores De Mayo, of course, made the Filipino organizers unhappy. But I did not care much what people said. I was focused on my conviction and there would be no turning back, for I had decided to follow my Lord.

In my life, I had never witnessed any baptism by immersion, neither did I have any clue as to how it was done. During Pastor Myrie's instructions, I learned of the significance and spiritual meaning, but as to its application, I knew nothing. Vic Inocencio, a fellow Filipino I came to know at the Mississauga Seventh-day Adventist Church, played his guitar and sang during my turn to go down to the pool. Maureen Stewart, a convert from the Pentecostal church, went in first. Although I knew what to do at the baptismal pool, it was overwhelmingly different from my imagination, especially in front of hundreds of curious church members.

I couldn't coordinate Pastor Myrie's instructions during our orientation. While Pastor Myrie was giving an introduction of me before the congregation, I repeatedly bent my knees, and he said: "We have a child of God here who can't wait anymore. She wants it over and done with." The congregation clapped in admiration of my excitement. My limbs were shaking, and I was wiping off my constant tears of inexplicable joy. I felt like I was floating in the air; there were these awesome songs in my ears seemingly coming from the voices of angels above who I knew were rejoicing for me, and I felt the presence of the Holy Spirit. I sincerely prayed that my family would experience this one day. From the very moment my feet touched the warm water of the baptismal pool, my joy overflowed. My tears of joy mingled with the water of the baptismal pool, as I triumphantly claimed by faith a new life in Christ. I could feel my closeness to my Lord and the inner joy surging in my heart. I thought I was floating in the air, as the church organ swelled and the congregation sang:

> "Ring the bells of heaven, there is joy today,
> For a soul returning from the wild.
> See the Father meets him out upon the way,
> Welcoming His weary wandering child.
> Glory, glory how the angels sing,
> Glory, glory how the loud harps ring;
> Tis the ransom army, like a mighty sea,
> Peeling forth the anthem of the free."

Minutes prior to my immersion, I looked at my family: Dexter, Brian, Christine, and Cathy, my eventual daughter-in-law. I felt so much joy knowing that my own family was attentive and watching, but I was saddened by the way they reacted. My husband, who had not shown up until the very last minute, would not stand when the pastor called my family to stand up and be recognized. He reluctantly stood up only after the repeated requests of the pastor. Yes, as I went under the water and came out, I heard the loud clapping of hands. When I looked at my family, they were overwhelmed too, I suppose. I was sure that they too, had never seen nor witnessed anything like this before. I watched the happy throng of God's family for one sinner to avail of the offered forgiveness and cleansing from sin, as symbolized by immersion into the water. It is symbolic of dying to self: buried in baptism, and rising into the newness of life by faith in Christ Jesus.

I can imagine the rapturous heavenly singing by the host of angels *"for a soul returning from the wild."* O what a feeling, of a soul set free having been redeemed by the blood of the Lamb! And Redeemed, how I love to proclaim it! The congregation kept singing until every newly baptized member had changed their respective baptismal gown into dry and warm clothing. I could imagine that the new robe of Christ's righteousness now covered me.

Pastor Myrie prayed the prayer of consecration. He prayed for us, the newly baptized. He petitioned heaven to write our names in the book of life, never more to be erased from there throughout eternity, while learning our early steps in our respective walk with the Lord. He prayed too that new believers would be met by persecution and trials as Jesus was. They need not be discouraged, as the Lord would always be with each of them, even to the end of the world.

How encouraging it was to become a member of the family of God on earth. Their hugs and handshakes were authentic and caring. On that Sabbath day, March 30, 2002, I found rest in Jesus and I came to Him Whose *yoke is easy and Whose burden is light.*

On our kitchen table at home there was a beautiful card and a bunch of gorgeous flowers from my children. In the card were my children's wishes, prayers, and congratulations for Mommy on the new faith that I had chosen. I had chosen to accept the Son of God as my Redeemer and Saviour, my faithful advocate on the day of judgment.

When I came to accept Jesus as my Lord and Saviour, it was to me a divinely recorded event, when in the name of Jesus, my Saviour, I willfully vowed and by faith chose to be buried with Him and be raised with Him to share His victory over sin.

FAMILY

My parents: Ernesto and Francisca

Standing before the remains of my 65-year-old childhood home during my visit to San Salvador Island, Philippines in 2015.

Nora Ednacot

My nursing school graduation photograph, taken in March 1974.

A photo of my husband, Tom, taken shortly after
his graduation from university.

Tom and me on our blessed wedding day, October 19, 1975.

My sons, Dexter and Brian, greeting their newborn
baby sister Christine in the hospital.

A snapshot of my young family at Christmas.

A photograph of my lovely family.

A treasured family photograph.

My family celebrating Christine's 13th birthday.

A high school graduation picture of my late son Brian.

My portrait.

A portrait of my family captured during a day of celebration: our silver wedding anniversary, Christine's 18th birthday, Dexter's graduation from university and Brian's lymphoma remission.

TANZANIA, AFRICA EVANGELISM 2005

The baptism of one of the 29 people that gave their lives to the Lord during my time in Tanzania with Share Him Global Evangelism.

Myself with the newly baptized Tanzanians.

Bringing the message to a Tanzanian crowd during the evangelistic series.

KIEV, UKRAINE EVANGELISM 2007

Expressing my humble gratitude to the Father during the baptismal service that concluded the three weeks of evangelism. My Ukrainian interpreter Katya stands to my right.

An image capturing my passionate delivery of the message of the Cross of Jesus to the congregation.

A baptismal candidate demonstrating that it is never too late to accept Jesus as Lord and Saviour.

Myself among church leaders and the newly baptized individuals.

MY LATE SON BRIAN

How can a mother ever forget the fruit of her womb? Such were the memories left by our late son, Brian, who was diagnosed with lymphoma when he was fifteen years old. As a mother and professional nurse, I knew the nature of this disease is quite difficult to deal with, that even in the field of medicine only a very minimal percentage of cases show that the afflicted patient survived, not to mention a lesser percentage of them who completely overcame.

When Brian's MRP doctors discussed their findings, they concluded that Brian's case was non-Hodgkin's lymphoma. The oncologist carefully explained to me Brian's prognosis, the possible consequences, the planned medical management, and probable surgeries. At the same time he gave me some glimmer of hope that the disease has a high cure rate. The soul of the mother inside me tried in vain to be brave against the painful possibilities slashing my heart. I tried to be brave, but the dark mantle of uncertainty lingered in my breast. I was searching for ways to share the matter with the members of my family.

Brian was my second son, a gift from God as precious as his brother Dexter. Looking at the face of my fifteen-year-old son, memories of his birth came flashing in my mind. It was on that balmy day of May 12,1978 when Brian first saw the light at Chedoke Hospital in Hamilton, Ontario. The varied fragrances of beautiful, colourful spring garden flowers like peonies, lilies, carnations, and orchids that I had never before seen were just blossoming. Having known the unexpected but well-received good news that our ten-month-old Dexter would soon become a big brother, Matt and I had at first prayed for a daughter. However, my personal bargaining with the Father had changed as the baby's arrival drew closer: "It does not matter, Lord, whether my womb would give me a boy or a girl as long as she/he is normal and shows no conspicuous physical deficiency, has a nose, two ears, four limbs, ten toes, ten fingers, and a mind to think." And as awesomely planned by the Lord, who knows our beginning and our end, the Great Designer had planned that Dexter's baby brother would arrive on Mother's Day. "A fitting gift for me" from the Father, I thought, on a day when mothers, grandmothers, and great-grandmothers are honoured by their children for their gifts of motherhood and maternal bonds.

Unknown to me, God, the designer and giver of life, must have felt jealous of me praising and thanking the wrong god and patron, instead of the true Creator. I was too innocent to thank the God that I did not know. As a mother, my heart was bursting with happiness.

A Bible passage written by God's servant King David acknowledges the realities of life: *"For you have formed my inward parts, You covered me in my mother's womb; I will praise you, for I am fearfully and wonderfully made. Marvelous are your works, and that my soul knows very well. My frame was not hidden from you. When I was made in secret, And skilfully wrought in the lowest part of the earth; Your eyes saw my substance, being yet unformed, And in your books they are all as written, The days fashioned for me, When as yet there were none of them"* (Psalm 139:13-16).

Had I known this truth from the beginning I should have sought after God and served Him, consecrated for Him my time and energy, rather than having wasted time in paying homage and sacrilege to the heathen idols and images. Yet the living God keeps loving everyone whether they acknowledge Him or not.

While sitting around the kitchen table with my three kids, our conversation picked up the idea of me becoming a grandmother like Grandma Taling, a woman who I can loudly and proudly declare was a one in a million mother-in-law. She loved her grandchildren very dearly and her sudden passing was from a one-time massive, mega stroke. In less than an hour she was gone. With the fleeting nature of time, our next moment is never guaranteed.

Dexter, with childhood confidence, said, "Mommy, I will give you two grandchildren." Christine said, "I will give Mommy two grandchildren," and she raised two little fingers. Brian said, "I will give Mommy three grandchildren, one like her," and I was moved. I thought I must be doing something right according to his young taste and young mind. But our darling Brian was not meant to become a father. At fifteen years old he was diagnosed with a slow and fatal disease. It started with a peculiar severe cough that lingered for weeks. It was so severe almost to the point of causing him to pass out due to his difficulty breathing during his bouts of coughing. Every night I kept a very close eye on Brian, for I feared that he might have a respiratory arrest from long episodes of coughing. I watched him ever carefully like a hawk, making sure that he was breathing and to reassure him that Mom is here beside him.

With his weight drastically dropping, we decided to bring Brian to St. Joseph Emergency Department. At St. Joseph he was given an initial CT Scan, then he was urgently transferred to Sick Kids Hospital for further medical management the following day. The final news regarding our fifteen-year-old boy only confirmed the initial diagnosis of non-Hodgkin's lymphoma. This news ripped apart my heart and devastated the well-being of Tom, Dexter, Christine, and Lola. I felt as if every part of me was shattered. As a nurse I knew that this disease is not only punishingly slow, but fatal and devastating for us who would be losing a son. Dexter and Christine would be losing a brother. Urgent surgery was performed on Brian to take out the clustered nodes that had irritated the airways and caused the severe coughing. For the next ten years, Brian fought gallantly a losing battle with lymphoma.

At sixteen, he attended a youth summer camp. There were various programs and sessions where campers would listen to a speaker and then follow up with certain activities. It was there that he felt he needed to write a letter to his parents.

In Brian's short and simple missive, one can perceive the kind of son he was. He grew to be a man and fought with heroic courage the debilitating non-Hodgkin's lymphoma.

During Brian's years of horrible struggle, I was also struggling. The battle between right and wrong was already raging in my soul: the forces of darkness versus the power of light. I had come to know the demands of the law and was trying to understand them in the light of my own narrow ways and flimsy concept of the personality and nature of God. Hence, when I read the first and second commandments, I was stalled. A terrible fear gripped my heart as I read what the second command of law says:

"You shall not make for yourself a carved image—any likeness of anything that is in heaven above, or that is in earth beneath, or that is in the water under the earth. You shall not bow down to them nor serve them, for I, the Lord your God, am a jealous God, visiting the iniquity of the fathers upon the children to the third and fourth generations of those who hate me, but showing mercy to thousands of those who love me and keep my commandments."

Simply reading this command gave me fear. I thought of my grandchildren. If Brian could have received the consequence of his grandparents' idolatry, then it could still happen to our Sidney and Max.

Nora Trims Her Lamp

EVERDEAREST MOM & DAD,   BREAKAWAY '95

    FIRST OF ALL, I WOULD LIKE TO LET YOU KNOW THAT I LOVE BOTH OF YOU VERY MUCH — MORE THAN YOU MAY THINK. WHEN HEARING THE SPEAKERS THIS WEEKEND TALK ABOUT THEIR RELATIONSHIPS W/ THEIR PARENTS, IT MADE ME REALIZE HOW TRULY LUCKY I HAVE BEEN AND ~~HOW BLESSED I HAVE BEEN~~ TO BE GIVEN SUCH A GREAT ~~FAMILY~~ & ESPECIALLY GREAT PARENTS. THE MAIN TOPIC THIS WEEKEND HAS BEEN ABOUT RELATIONSHIPS. A FEW ~~TEENAGERS~~ SPOKE & SHARED ABOUT THEIR TROUBLED RELATIONSHIPS WITH THEIR ~~PARENTS~~ WHICH MADE ME TO STOP & THANK GOD FOR GIVING ME YOU!

    I KNOW THAT YOU DON'T HEAR ME OFTEN SAY THAT "I LOVE YOU" BECAUSE I DON'T OFTEN SAY IT. BUT I KNOW THAT YOU KNOW THAT I DO LOVE YOU WITH ALL OF MY HEART AND I WANT TO THANK YOU FOR EVERYTHING THAT YOU HAVE DONE FOR ME IN THIS 16 YEAR & 11 MONTH LIFE OF MINE. I WANT TO THANK YOU BOTH FOR EVERYTHING YOU HAVE DONE FOR ME FROM DRIVING ME TO MY BASEBALL GAMES TO TAKING CARE OF ME & PRAYING FOR ME WHILE I HAVE BEEN SICK.

    I KNOW THAT THERE HAVE BEEN TIMES WHERE I HAVE HURT YOUR FEELINGS EITHER BY SOMETHING I SAID OR SOMETHING I DIDN'T SAY BUT I WANT BOTH OF YOU TO KNOW THAT I APOLOGIZE FOR ALL OF THE TIMES I HAVE HURT YOU AND ASK YOU TO FORGIVE ME. FORGIVE ME FOR THE TIMES THAT I HAVE BEEN UNFAITHFUL TO YOU, TOOK ADVANTAGE OF YOU AND EMOTIONALLY HURT YOUR FEELINGS.

    I WOULD ALSO LIKE TO THANK YOU FOR GIVING ME THE OPPORTUNITY TO COME TO THIS BREAKAWAY RETREAT. AT FIRST, I DIDN'T REALLY WANT TO COME BECAUSE I WOULD HAVE RATHER SPENT THE WEEKEND WITH MY FRIENDS BUT COMING TO THIS HAS MADE ME REALIZE MANY THINGS LIKE HOW LUCKY I AM TO HAVE YOU & HOW MUCH I LOVE YOU BOTH.

    SEE YOU SOON! I LOVE YOU BOTH!

                                  LOVE ALWAYZ,

Our marriage had suffered. Over time, Matt had chosen to be with his friends more than with me. When I eventually decided to separate from their father, Brian had already been gone for about eight years. Dexter burst into anger. He blamed "MY GOD". He swore at me and used unforgivable words in anger. I told him that for his disrespect and dishonour to me, his mother, he was bound to receive severe consequences from God. Out of my deep hurt, I said it may not be him who will be the recipient of the penalty - it may be his children. And this is why they said that I was casting death on their newborn Max. My children misunderstood me to be one who is courting death and casting a curse on the family. For that I was forbidden to ever step foot into my son's house. I was told not to come near their children, ever.

But in my sorrow and longing I disobeyed without them knowing it. I drove on late winter nights to their place with my head and face well-covered with a scarf and parked my car just close enough to see their shadows. By being close to them, I tried to relieve my saddened heart and tears. Many early mornings I parked my car just close enough so that I could catch a glimpse of my dear grandchildren as they left the house for school.

It is dangerous to self interpret and make a conclusion about the scripture as it is read, and not as the Bible would interpret itself. Doing so will misconstrue the eternal loving character of God. It was only after I had languished in my agony in fear and sorrow that I was given a comforting and relieving light of understanding from a passionate Bible teacher. The explanation lies in knowing and understanding God.

"The jealous God visits the iniquity of parents unto their children from third and fourth generations." He is jealous because of the sad effect when parents deny the One True God who created us, but instead worship the false gods made and engraved by human hands. This disrespect of the One True God can be carried and inherited until the third and fourth generations, and these generations will be in danger of reaping the evil consequences of their deeds. Whereas when parents show fidelity to God, their children also have the blessed opportunity of knowing and being blessed by God.

With the help of the Holy Spirit Who gives understanding, I begin to grasp that God's law must serve as a hedge to prevent mankind's total separation from God. God's law is a law of love and not of a punitive god of hate. Our God is a jealous God. The prophet Jeremiah testified: *"The Lord has appeared of old to me saying: 'Yes, I have loved you with an everlasting love; therefore with loving kindness I have drawn you'"* (Jer. 31:3). Our God is not pleased at being separated from His children. Why should God punish the children for the iniquity of the fathers? God is jealous of His great desire for His children's well-being. The law does not say God will punish the children, although some versions imply that. Instead, the law states that the iniquity of the parents can hurt their children down to the third and fourth generations. The Bible says, "He visits the iniquity of the fathers upon their children," meaning that He can remember and recall an account of the iniquity of the parents and the impact of their iniquities to their children, down to the third and fourth generations. God is jealous, for the children can easily be influenced by their parents' misdeeds. Hence, God offers His mercy to the thousands of them who love Him. As John the Apostle wrote:

"If we confess our sins, He is faithful and just to forgive us our sins and to cleanse us from all unrighteousness" (1John 1:9). And, further John said: *"My little children, these things I write to you, so that you may not sin. And if anyone sins, we have an advocate with the Father, Jesus Christ, the Righteous" (1John 2:1).*

The Law of God should serve as a loving warning, for He does not want any to perish, but all should come to repentance (2 Peter 3:9). He longs to show mercy to the repentant sinner as He is merciful to the thousands of them who love Him.

It was during Brian's final admission at Princess Margaret Hospital when my heart was so compelled to speak about Jesus. For many days I prayed for courage and guidance to guide my lips as I talked to my son. I requested a "no visitors except mother" sign. Prayerfully, I asked my boy, "My son, if Jesus would come next week, who is your Lord and Saviour?"

Brian categorically replied, "Mom, He is Jesus. Jesus is the Lord!" He said this with a firm voice. Then looking straight at me, he asked in return, "Mom, weren't you listening in the church?"

"Thank you, son, that's all I wanted to know." I walked to the washroom, my joy overflowing. I cried to God with tears of inexplicable joy for the triumph of His love, "Now give my son rest until the blessed morning. May your will be done."

The doctor came to discuss Brian's code status, and my son bravely and willingly consented to DNR. My son looked at me while speaking with the doctor. He implored with his eyes, "Mom, I am tired, please let me go when the time comes."

During the funeral of his Aunt Conching, Brian insisted that he accompany me to pay his respects also. At that time he could hardly step in and out of the car and he needed the aid of a wheelchair. It was just Mommy and Brian in the car to the cemetery. There was a deathly silence in the car. Every moment that our eyes met, we both knew that his turn was forthcoming; we were aware that he too would be laid to rest like his auntie. Oh, how I was hurting. Many of my tears were shed not for Aunt Conching but for what I foresaw: I myself would soon be wearing a black dress and laying flowers on a grave.

I was overshadowed by a mantle of gloom. I recalled how he and his big brother had been stars of their baseball team several years earlier. I had been one of those mothers who shouts and yells in the baseball field:

"That's my boy! That's Nora's boy!" Dexter's winning home run and stealing of bases made a superb performance. His three or four shoulder dislocations fixed by surgery did not stop him from playing with the Marauders Baseball roster of McMaster University. Dexter could run, he could hit, he could throw the ball from the outfield fence right to the catcher's glove to the letter. Brian was not as muscular as Dexter, yet he was smoothly artistic in his moves while catching or throwing the ball.

I took pride as a mother in the number of trophies, plaques, and medals that all my children collected throughout those years of academic and athletic excellence attested by their sterling performances. There was a time when I took a day off from work to wash off dust from their accumulated trophies that completely covered our fireplace mantel. I remember positioning the collection on our backyard picnic table, soaping each one of them, then using a garden hose to rinse them off while standing up on a chair.

I have good and precious memories of the days when Tom and I invested our energy and time into our children. We never resented this time, as we knew our children would not get involved in any wrongdoings. But now, right before my eyes was my boy, so emaciated from his advanced debilitating disease that he could hardly stretch his legs any longer. His food swallowing was progressively deteriorating.

The evening of October 12, 2004 we had to rush Brian to Trillium Hospital Emergency Room. His difficulty in breathing had brought the family into a panic. I knew Christine's *Kuya* Brian was no longer coming back to the house. As Dexter carried his baby brother to the car, it was to be his final lift and embrace to a dying brother. Before I closed the door I fell to my knees, sobbing. I said, "Great God, this is it." I knew our Brian would not walk through this door ever again.

Everything went fast in the emergency unit. Brian was intubated and ventilated. The Lord in His mercy allowed a chance that my once baby boy and his mom would have a final look, a farewell to each other before the heavy sedation took effect prior to his transfer to ICU. The lounge became like a camping ground filled with sorrowing and broken-hearted friends and relatives. They all stood by their parting loved one.

In the intensive care unit, it was hoped that he would turn around for the better through all possible inotropic infusions to get his heart working, but one by one they could only do so much. Even the ventilator setting was utilized at its maximum, a 100% oxygen level that meant his respiratory system had shut down. The volume of the intravenous fluids given to get his failing kidneys working grossly disfigured my son, who had been the handsomest little darling in his junior kindergarten class.

I laboured with Brian all those ten long years. He felt our love and the love of his family, friends, and relatives. That moment when Brian confidently said his Lord is Jesus was very assuring to me, and I knew that Jesus would surely remember him come resurrection day.

Our filial love made us grieve deeply for the demise of Brian. His siblings were devastated, as were we, his parents. I suffered long before I was able to move on. Every now and then the weight of the burden seemed to return. But thanks be to the God of life and restoration, believing Christians should not give too much attention to the temporary but to what Jesus taught: focus more on the things that will last to eternity. When Christ was still ministering on this earth, He laboured towards pointing the people to behold the things that are of eternal importance.

To true believing Christians, death is not the end of all things. The Lord's promises in the Bible provided me with the comfort and solace that my aching heart needed. The new hope this comfort brought made me compare death to entering a chamber to change one's dress for an awaited grand occasion, to meet in person the greatest being of all time - Jesus. Listen to the Apostle Paul:

"Behold I tell you a mystery: We shall not all sleep, but we shall all be changed—in a moment, in the twinkling of an eye, at the last trumpet. For the trumpet will sound, and the dead will be raised incorruptible, and we shall all be changed. For this corruptible must put on incorruptible, and this mortal must put on immortality. So when this corruptible has put on incorruptible, and this mortal has put on immortality, then shall be brought to pass the saying that is written: Death is swallowed up in victory! O death where is your sting? O grave where is your victory?" (1Corinthians 15:51-56).

This promise gave me comfort and assurance of seeing Brian again, who would be completely changed into the glorious body without corruption to live forever. My darling daughter Christine rendered a very fitting song as she bid goodbye to her Kuya:

> *"When peace, like a river, attendeth my way,*
> *When sorrows like sea billows roll*
> *Whatever my lot, Thou hast taught me to say,*
> *It is well, it is well with my soul.*
> *My sin – O the bliss of this glorious thought!*
> *My sin not in part, but the whole,*
> *Is nailed to the cross and I bear it no more*
> *Praise the Lord, praise the Lord, O my soul."*

Carried by her strong emotion, Christine's voice stammered a bit and her lips quivered, but she courageously went on to finish her song:

> *"And, Lord, haste the day when my faith shall be sight*
> *The clouds be rolled back as the scroll;*
> *The trump shall resound and the Lord shall descend*
> *Even so, It is well with my soul."*

OUR DEAREST BRIAN

Brian Thomas is the forever dearest late little brother of Dexter, big brother of Christine, and much loved brother-in-law of Catherine.

Sydney and Max, the two adorable little ones of Dex and Cathy, were born not too long after Brian's passing. They are the niece and nephew that Brian never had the chance to cuddle nor swing in his arms. Brian was not there to sing for them "Twinkle, twinkle little star" nor "Jesus loves me this I know". He could not tickle or kiss their teeny weeny toes and feet for fun and laughter, nor could he chase them around the house for hide and seek. He was not there to play a peek-a-boo game. Their late Uncle Brian never had the chance to give them a goodnight kiss, a great big tight tight hug and embrace, nor a final goodbye before his passing. He could not speak words of goodbye such as "Be good to Mommy and Daddy; love them and be obedient to them; finish school; at Jesus feet we shall meet each other again one day."

Max and Sydney do not have anything to recollect about late Uncle Brian. They have no happy memories to recall of a lost uncle. And when they reach an age to understand life, still they will not be able to relate to the grief, sorrow, and pain their father Dexter, Auntie Christine, Grandpa Matt, and Great Grandma Taling went through. They will not understand the tears shed for years by their aging Grandma Nora.

It took me a long time before I could speak about our dear son in past tense. I used to choke and my tongue would become twisted on very many occasions, for many long years.

In the event of fire, my most precious possessions that I would bring to safety above anything else are three treasured family portraits hanging on our living room walls. Each person in these portraits has a story of his or her own to unfold.

Matt is God's gift to me as my life partner who I swore to love and to cherish in sickness and in health that not one stranger will I allow to come between us, come what may, in whatever circumstances life brings.

Our first child Dexter is but one story to tell, beginning with my very first birthing experience in the Philippines in my young maternal role.

Our dear Christine Charise is our dream come true for having a daughter, a gift granted by the Lord. Christine was born when Brian was four. At the age of seven she learned how to sing, and in her brother's final hours she delivered her trembling but most awesome soprano voice to honour her brother with "It is Well with My Soul".

Always, there is our Brian Thomas, the reason for this chapter. Yes, now and again I experience flashing memories of our Brian, the key to my finding the ultimate need of man, The Everlasting Almighty God in His Son's most awesome and irrefutably controversial and disputed name Christ Jesus without Whom life would be lifeless, hopeless, and meaningless.

It was God's plan executed by His begotten Son, when on that sixth day of creation man was formed according to His own likeness. The first human was meticulously crafted by the holy hand of God patterned in his likeness, without defects nor any inkling to disobey. Male and female God created them, until sin brought by an enemy marred the tranquil atmosphere in the Eden home of the first couple. Sin brought discord and all the maladies in the world. But the Son of God volunteered to execute the Rescue Plan, the Plan of Salvation. He was willing to give His immaculate life for the redemption of mankind.

What mother would not smile as her son comes home after his very first day of school with a beaming smile, for he can no longer contain his awesome news: "Mommy, Daddy, did you know that I am the handsomest in the class?"

We had a big laugh over it. And Matt, his Dad said, "Good for you, son, for staying humble." Such a fond moment won't be easily negated by caring parents. Other parents would even go to the extent of being provoked by the slightest misrepresentation of others upon their young.

My thumbs went up to acknowledge our darling boy's announcement. As parents we fondly shared this story with our friends and relatives who expressed fondness for our son. He was an affectionate child full of promise and energy. How could I ever forget those moments when he would sit on my lap, stroking my face to get attention, then extend his arms wide and say, "Mommy, I love you this much."

Brian was about seven and Christine was three when one evening, while the whole family was watching a T.V. commercial for beautiful wedding gowns, Christine out of the blue stood up and started twirling before us all and announced: "Mommy,

Daddy, when I get married…" she paused when her protective brother Brian also stood up, with his hands on his waist, and interrupted her: "Christine, you cannot even go to the washroom by yourself yet…what's more get married." The mother's heart in me cannot resist smiling from remembering these funny moments of her little ones.

Brian was a curious and smart little boy. I asked him one time to vacuum the carpet, first informing him that he would be compensated with a quarter after the work was done. Shaking his head like an adult, he approached me and said, "Such a hard job Mommy, for just a quarter?"

Mr. Smith, a young teacher at St. Matthews, later moved to Xavier to teach high school. He gave me a surprise call to meet with him at the school cafeteria. The appointment was scheduled to take place in four days, and my apprehension gave me some sleepless nights in fear what my children might have done wrong at school. When the day came Mr. Smith's opening line was, "Mrs. Brozo, I am getting married."

"So?" was my surprised response.

Mr. Smith, very composed and relaxed, continued, "What is your secret with your children, Mrs. Brozo? The conduct of Dexter, Brian, and Christine was always ideal throughout elementary school and high school. I want to raise a family soon after my fiancée and I get married."

After Brian's diagnosis, the fear of the unknown was killing both of us. I have loved my children equally, but somehow Brian appeared closer, for who else would he best turn to but his mother? Many nights he would come to our bed. He would speak not a word, but his silence spoke a thousand words - what now, Mom? What is next, Mom?

How can a mother's heart not be split into pieces when her boy falls on his knees weeping, asking "Mommy, am I going to die?" Ever so desperate, a wise answer came to me from the fountain of wisdom and an unknown power guided my lips to calm my son.

I said, "Man's life is similar to a lighted candle. There are candles that burn fast and there are candles that burn slow. There are those whose lights snuff out as soon as they are lighted, there those whose lights remain longer, and there still others that keep burning until the flame reaches the floor before their flames disappear."

In the chapel at Sick Children's Hospital, I lay face down on the floor, arms apart, and in humility begged God for a miracle healing. I did not mind the stares of those who were seated for I was there to discuss a serious matter with the merciful and loving God.

Our lost boy surely must have prayed to God intently at one point or another, that I know. Brian wrote a very simple but appealing letter to God the Father in Jesus' name on the night before his very first surgery at Sick Children's Hospital. The operating room nurse allowed him to carry the precious note in his hands to the operating room. In his letter he begged the Lord for a miracle, that he would survive the surgery. He asked for God's grace to live for more years and fulfill his dream of becoming a kinesiologist one day.

On countless occasions I did not only engage in dialogue with the Father, but I also argued with Him face-to-face so to speak. After all, His invitation in the Book of Isaiah 1:18 asks us to come and let us reason together. I questioned God why this happened to our boy. In my selfishness I asked, "Why him? Why a promising young man?" when there were many others who do not value their lives. Why did this happen to our son, who, from the best of my knowledge had not caused any school misconduct, who had not caused anyone any intentional harm, who was a friend to many both in school and outside of school, who was the joy of any teacher to have in their class? Yes, our Brian had never thrown any dishonouring or disrespectful words to us, his parents, that could have gone unnoticed by the ears of God. But no matter what questions I raised with God, His divine decision and plan are still for our best.

Brian bravely went through the Autologous Bone Marrow Transplant at Toronto General Hospital when he turned eighteen. The protocol of this surgery was extremely intensive with mega high doses of chemotherapy. It is only by God's grace that he came through it at all, and after ten days he was discharged and allowed to return home.

The disease progressed in spite of the transplant. Still, chemo and radiation went on. With needle pokes everywhere, his arms became pincushions. Brian was given blood transfusions one after another with all kinds of central lines - for he eventually ran out of peripheral veins. He was subjected to repeated chest surgeries, pain medications, anti-vomiting drugs, hair loss, weight loss, and peculiar face swelling from mega doses of cortisone. Above all, he missed his schoolmates and his school.

There were countless, long, lonely, devastating nights of pain and misery for Brian. There was nothing, nothing at all that our son did not have to endure. He persevered through it all so bravely, and his family and friends were with him all the way.

Dexter and Christine never stopped spending time with their ever dearest brother who they very well knew would be leaving them soon. On his good days they would take Brian to the mall in his wheelchair accompanied by a portable oxygen tank.

I gave my word to Brian that became a favourite line for the family: "Mom is going to the moon to sell toothpicks." Yes, I promised that I would do all that was within my capacity, even if I had to go to the moon and sell toothpicks to raise money for his oncology treatment in the U.S. Of course there was no toothpick selling on the moon, but I worked double time, I borrowed money from the bank, and we brought Brian to Beth Israel Hospital in Boston, U.S. for a week of treatment on an outpatient arrangement. The treatment was supposed to give Brian a 75% cure rate. After all, who would not do anything and everything under the sun for their ailing child?

Walking distance from the hospital, Brian and I occupied a room in a very well-equipped and highly renovated house for its purpose. This establishment was coordinated and run by social workers. The beautiful house was donated by one very kind, generous, and affluent family whose young daughter had died of brain cancer. Through prayers and God's guidance, we had been led to find this place where the accommodation cost was just a voluntary donation. While receiving treatment, a cancer patient could stay in this house with one family member. Some would come from different countries to receive the highly researched and well-documented treatment at Beth Israel Hospital. We went there hoping and praying that what the hospital offered would cure or at least buy time for our loved one. But we knew that cancer is cancer, and death would come.

Brian was the youngest resident, the baby in the house. We all bonded quickly, with each person very much humbled by our reasons for coming. Some families couldn't help but shed tears almost every morning at the kitchen table. Some had run out of tears to shed; my own tear ducts had gone dry. We shared our pain and our eyes spoke our fears of what was imminent: that the loved one we had brought for treatment had but a little time left. We gave each other hugs like we had known each other for a long time. There were about three or four of us who went regularly to the nearby church to pray even for few minutes. We knelt and spoke as one. We begged God as one family, united by the same need for help from the Maker to sustain our beloved and hold them through their ordeal.

On his third day of treatment, Brian became septic from his central line on his right subclavian vein. He experienced occasional but very severe and vigorous chills. The only relief was to have very hot water run over his chilled body in the shower. As Brian would turn blue, I would plead and pray earnestly to God. One evening, in a panic, I became vocal to God - so vocal that in the time of Moses I could have been easily struck down to death in the blink of an eye. "Dear merciful and most loving Father, if you are to take him, please God…" cried my trembling voice. With tears, sobs, and Brian listening, I said, "…not in the shower room, dear Father of heaven."

With the severe chills recurring every two to three hours, I was losing my mind. Repeated events brought Brian and I into panic one evening when he experienced such severe chills that the bed was shaking. I had the blow dryer to the maximum heat to give him the comfort that his whole body demanded. In a panic I set the water to a much hotter temperature and he remained under the hot water for much longer than previous times, so long that I feared he might end up with burns. I had no choice but call 911 and have him admitted to the hospital.

But we had to come home. Our funds ran out because of the unexpected sky high ICU admission billing. Matt and his brother came to pick us up in Boston and we returned back to Toronto General Hospital. I monitored his intravenous and antibiotics during the drive. We said goodbye forever to all the residents and their families before we left. Through our sadness the tears did not stop flowing, for we all knew that none of us would ever come to meet each other again given the situation and the distance in this sin-sick planet Earth.

As a nurse, I have looked after several dying patients, both young and old. No matter what, nurses have soft spots in their hearts. They can be so moved to tears that they cry with their patients and their grieving families. I once knelt in the washroom before God in prayer, as I begged the Lord for his mercy and grace on my thirty-three-year-old male patient who had suddenly coded from a massive heart attack. "Lord, please deliver this man;" was my sincere plea, "you can use him for your vineyard."

I once had a nightmare over the most beautiful curly haired seven-year-old girl patient on the pediatric floor. The nurses and the doctors were speechless and very much saddened for we could not execute her body's demand to survive. All we could do was just watch and wait until she breathed her last breath, because of the family's religious belief for no blood transfusion - no matter how, no matter what.

Yes, death, the sting of death, that was never in God's agenda in the beginning. Jesus is the Sustainer of life; Jesus the source of life. Yes, Jesus calls the dead to life, the dead into living. I wanted just a few more minutes of life for my dearest boy so that I could give him my final embrace, give him my sweetest kiss, say my final but temporary goodbye, for I whispered in his ears, that one day, in Jesus' name I said, "You and me will see each other again." In my shattered voice I expressed my sorrow to my boy. "Sorry, my dear son, for anything that I as your mother could have done more of or better, or if I missed doing anything knowingly or otherwise, please forgive me, my dearest darling," was my uttering.

Yes, letting go of my dearest boy was way beyond anything we had ever before experienced. Matt and I had to retreat and allow our once bundle of joy to lay at rest. I had to let go of the flesh of my flesh that God had given me, but I selfishly held on for so long. Our dear Father, who very well knows what is best for us all, beyond the shadow of a doubt, had to finally withdraw the breath of life he had loaned to our Brian Thomas for twenty-five years.

WHAT HAPPENS TO A SOUL AT DEATH?

As a former member of the mystical religion of Romanism, I used to believe that the soul of the righteous person goes to heaven in three days. I had no knowledge as to what they would be doing in heaven or in what form they would assume existence. What if the person who died was not righteous? Well, his soul would go straight to hell. But the same church taught us that those who were not so sinful nor so righteous would remain wallowing in purgatory until they were bailed out by prayers of their loved ones and through the sponsorship of saints. I couldn't find assurance in these old answers. The simplistic answers were from naysayers and traditions of men, and they only invited more questions. These answers did not align with the whole picture of the nature of man after death.

The Holy Spirit reminds me that it is always dangerous to follow the teachings made by man. The Bible and God alone can give sure unerring answers. It is here that I have found comforting answers to my own questions. What happens when man dies? What is the truth about those who have died? My thoughts lingered in uncertainties until I read the word of God, and read the assurance of Jesus Who said, *"I am the resurrection and the life" (John 11:25)*.

With my Bible in hand and the Holy Spirit's guidance, I remembered Pastor Adap's teaching that "it is good to consider the beginning of life to help us understand how it ends." What elements constituted the first man when he was created? Genesis 2:7 provides an answer, saying: *"And the Lord, God, formed man of the dust of the ground, and breathed into his nostrils the breath of life; and man became a living soul."* Now we see a picture and the composition of the first living soul: he was dust of the ground, formed in the image of God, and was given *breath of life*. That was the first human, called a living soul. It's the addition of the breath from the life-giving God that makes the dust alive.

What happens at death? Proverbs 12:7 has an answer:

"Then the dust will return to the earth as it was, and the spirit (breath of life) will return to God Who gave it." At death, the reversal of the beginning takes place. This teaches me that there is no immediate assumption of heaven after death, neither is there resurrection, except maybe in special cases mentioned in the Bible. The point here I understand is that this body of dust goes back to the earth and the breath returns to the giver.

Is the soul immortal that it does not die? Again, the Bible has an answer ready: "*A soul that sins, it shall die*" (Ezekiel 18:4). Even the thoughts and the memories are present no longer. Psalms 146:4 explains that the (spirit) breath of life departs, the body returns to the earth, and his thoughts (plans) perish. Even the feelings and emotions die with man when he dies. Eccl.9:5 states that *"their love, and their hate and their envy already perished."*

We can hope for something better for those who have accepted the Lordship of Jesus in their lives. If you would ask Jesus, He would illustrate death to you in a very comforting manner, for He sees the death of His friends just as if they were sleeping. Referring to His friend Lazarus, He said: "Our friend Lazarus sleeps, but I go that I might wake Him up" (John 11:11).

So, when is the general resurrection going to happen, if not on the third day as many have supposed? The Bible answers that question with unfailing assurance: *"For the Lord Himself will descend from heaven with a shout, with the voice of an archangel, and with the trumpet of God, and the dead in Christ will rise first. Then we who are alive and remain shall be caught up together with them in the clouds to meet the Lord in the air. And thus we shall always be with the Lord. Therefore, comfort one another with these words"* (1Thess. 4:16-18).

It was very comforting for me to know that my Brian rested in a peaceful sleep with an assurance of going back to life without lymphoma, perfected in the image of His Saviour. He is in the grave as yet. I will see him on that blessed resurrection morning. The Lord of life does not want us to be ignorant of these things. Apostle Paul said: *"But I do not want you to be ignorant, brethren, concerning those who have fallen asleep, lest you sorrow as others who have no hope. For if we believe that Jesus died and rose again, even so God will bring with Him those who sleep in Jesus, for this we say to you by the word of the Lord, that we, who are alive or remain until the coming of the Lord will by no means precede those who are asleep"* (1 Thess. 4:13-15).

Jesus is the resurrection and the life. He promised to bring life again to those who died in His name.

Job the Patriarch expressed his firm grip of God's word when he declared: *"For I know that my Redeemer lives and He shall stand at last on the earth. And after my skin is destroyed, this I know, that in my flesh I shall see God"* (Job 19:25-26).

What a precious assurance. This mortal body shall wait until that moment when, in a twinkling of an eye, Jesus shall come and with the voice of an archangel call the dead to put on immortality. I can imagine that the grave is just like entering a closet to change our old garment of destruction into the eternal glorious garb of immortality.

BLESSED ASSURANCE TO A BELIEVER

After Jesus' baptism, he fasted for forty days and forty nights and was weakened by hunger. That is when the tempter came to tempt Him.

Satan's strategy was shown in his attempt to derail Jesus from His mission. First, the devil tried to sow seeds of doubt in Jesus, saying: "If you are the Son of God, command that these stones become bread" (Matthew 4:4 NKJV).

The prince of darkness and unrighteousness, the devil, will do the same unto new believers, to make them doubt their having accepted the Lord Jesus as their Saviour. He will plant seeds of uncertainty and let them vacillate in their newfound faith. Satan would not allow anybody to abandon his camp without a fight. He will do every possible thing he's been allowed to do. What then is the assurance for one who is new in the faith and a fledgling believer like me, against such a wily foe that is called the devil? If those who were long in the faith are still struggling with difficulties, then how much more can new believers expect? Jesus said that the battle is the Lord's. Let us abide in His triumphant camp. Holy men of God, like Moses, Joshua, David, and others, knew how to fight the winning fight, because they believed that the battle is the Lord's. Jesus has defeated Satan, and he could not snatch believers from Jesus' love.

Satan knows that God's children are formidable as long as they fight the fight of faith. At Calvary, Jesus sealed the victory of every sinner who came to Him by faith and gained victory with Him. The Devil knew that his defeat was certain and his lies had been uncovered. He could not kill Jesus the second time, but he could make the compassionate Jesus feel badly. So, the devil and all his hosts are set on causing untold sufferings and troubles upon the children of God. Then Satan tempts God's children by making them doubt the love of God, and think that their God has abandoned them.

The prince of darkness will do everything that could make God feel sad and unhappy. For God feels the pain that his children feel. It is Satan who makes us feel bad and suffer bad things, because he wants to inflict sadness upon God. Satan wants to see Jesus cry with those who are crying, and suffer with those who are suffering.

Can we see the tears in the voice of Jesus as recorded in the Gospel of Matthew, who wrote: *"Then Jesus expressed His longing for His people, saying, 'O Jerusalem, how much I care about you, even if you have killed the prophets. I long to protect you from what is coming, just as a mother hen protects her chicks and covers them with her wings. But you are too proud and indifferent to listen. Soon your temple will be emptied of God's presence'" (Matthew 23:37,38 TCW).*

I languished long and deep during my days of my spiritual blindness. I fought the battle all by my impulsive self. My knowledge of the supernatural foe was based on fictions and faulty imagination. I am since done with this, as I have learned the love of my personal Saviour and God. Their presence is now real within my soul. Just listen to this assurance from the Apostle Paul:

> *If God is for us, who can ever be against us?*
> *Since God did not spare even His own Son, but gave Him up for us all, won't God, Who gave us Christ also give us everything else?*
> *Who dares accuse us whom God has chosen for His own? Will God? No! He is the One who has given us right standing with Himself. Who then will condemn us? Will Christ Jesus? No, for He is the One Who died for us and was raised to life and is sitting at the place of highest honour next to God, pleading for us.*
> *Can anything ever separate us from Christ's love?*
> *Does it mean He no longer loves us if we have trouble or calamity, or are persecuted, or are hungry or cold, or are in danger or threatened with death? (Even the scripture says, "For your sake we are killed every day, we are being slaughtered like sheep") No, despite all these things, overwhelming victory is ours through Christ who loved us. (Romans 8:31-37 NIV)*

My heart sings for joy in my newfound faith. I am beginning an altogether new journey. I have found a friend in Jesus, Who has assured me of His supporting presence. Yet being new in the faith, I am craving spiritual maturity which Jesus would like me to have by facing the realities of everyday living, one day at a time. Jesus has proven to me His eternal love and unrelenting patience to help me learn more about life and of Him who is the Way, the Truth, and the Life.

My family was present when I was baptized, but they were not happy about it. They were oblivious of the joys that I received from my Saviour Jesus. They had not tasted the goodness of God. Their eyes remained blind and missed the visions of glory I was beholding. My husband Tom, my sons Dexter and Brian, and my daughter Christine, and Cathy, Dexter's girlfriend who became my daughter-in-law, were present to witness my baptism when I embraced the truth the Holy Scripture teaches. To show his disappointment, my husband refused to stand up and be recognized by the congregation. I have kept this incident in my heart and I am praying that the Lord will open their hearts in due time to hear the still small voice of God.

The enemy of the soul had a firm grip upon Tom, drawing him yet further away. He did not come home until very late that night. He was very angry at me for giving up the old beliefs I had before I had met him, and for embracing the faith of Jesus with the Seventh-day Adventist Christians. Tom repeatedly denounced Adventists as belonging to a cult and bragged that one day he would prove to me that the Adventists' teachings are wrong. His disappointment was aggravated when I decided to throw away four boxes containing fifty-two statues and images. My family thought I was losing my mind, and even considered calling a priest to exorcise me and indoctrinate me anew. In God's mercy He provided them time to mellow their angry hearts before they could make any crazy moves.

I struggled the most with my Sabbath observance. The temptations of physical and personal convenience were blocking me. Satan offered me good, fat compensation for every Saturday overtime hour in my job. Before I was baptized I used to go partying, dancing, playing cards, and playing *mah-jong* on Saturdays. I had to let these things go and let God take control. Praise God, He changed my tastes and preferences. I became aware that I had been called for a reason, and by His Spirit He helped me grow in the grace and in the knowledge of my Lord and Saviour, Jesus Christ. I grew in my acquaintance with God, who I now addressed as My eternal loving God, "My Father".

I kept wondering about the indifference that had enslaved my family, but I could only bring this to God in prayer. Sherry Grossett was a God-sent friend who encouraged me to hang on to God's promise in Hebrews 10:35,36: *"Therefore do not cast away your confidences, which has great reward. For you have need of endurance, so that after you have done the will of God, you may receive the promise."*

Bible truths are indeed amazing. I had been blinded and deceived by my former religious upbringing, of believing that good works and more good works were what it takes to retain or win the love of God. I didn't realize then how simply the Bible puts it. The Apostle Paul says the truth: *"But God demonstrates His own love towards us, in that while we were yet sinners, Christ died for us" (Romans 5:8)*. We cannot add nor subtract nor reverse the situation. It was God who first loved us because when we were yet sinners, Jesus died for us. This declaration from God is so inspiring.

Thousands, and even millions, have the wrong idea that in order to please God one needs to serve Him the best he can. Fear of His wrath drives them to do penance and inflict themselves with severe hardship to show penitence and repentance. But it is not the will of God that we inflict or cause pain to the body which is the temple of the Holy Spirit. Fear is not love. John, the beloved disciple, testified by saying: *"Love has been perfected among us in this; that we may have boldness in the day of judgment; because as He is, so are we in this world. There is no fear in love; perfect love casts out fear; because fear involves torment. But he who fears has not been made perfect in love. We love Him, because He first loved us"* (1 John 4:17-19). So, what happens to those whose allegiance to God is motivated by fear? The Bible says that those who fear have not been perfected in love. Therefore their worship and service to God are void and meaningless.

The government of God is founded in love, hence love is the fulfillment of the law. Look at the law in the context of love and you'll find it very comforting. This is why those who have fallen in love with Jesus and claim Him as their Saviour can say out of their love that Jesus is everything. For Jesus according to the Bible is the revelation of God.

My new Friend has time and again given me encouragement when I am tired and heavily tested, such as this verse from Jeremiah 32:17: *"Ah, Lord God! Behold you have made the heavens by your great power and outstretched arms, there is nothing too hard for you."* Jeremiah 32:27 also says, *"Behold, I am the Lord, the God of all flesh. Is there anything too hard for me?"*

I completely believe. God said it, and I believe it. In His own good time He will work His will for my loved ones. In a little while this journey will be over. Now, I long to see the fullness of the lights at the end of my life's trail. In the gospel of John 15:15,16, Jesus said: *"I no longer call you servants, because a master does not confide in his servants. Now you are my friends since I have told you everything the Father told me. You didn't choose me, I chose you. I appointed you to go and produce fruit that will last, so that the Father will give you whatever you ask for using my name."*

Songwriter John M. Scriven (1820-1886) conveyed his sentiment and friendship with Jesus in a song he wrote in 1855 entitled *"What a Friend We Have in Jesus"*:

> *What a friend we have in Jesus, all our sins and grief to bear;*
> *What a privilege to carry everything to God in prayer!*
> *O what peace we often forfeit, O what needless pain we bear,*
> *All because we do not carry everything to God in prayer.*
>
> *Have we trials and temptation, Is there trouble anywhere?*
> *We should never be discouraged, take it to the Lord in prayer!*
> *Can we find a friend so faithful, Who will all our sorrow share?*
> *Jesus knows our every weakness; Take it to the Lord in prayer!*
>
> *Are we weak and heavy laden, cumbered with a load of care?*
> *Precious Saviour still our refuge, Take it to the Lord in prayer!*
> *Do thy friends despise, forsake thee? Take it to the Lord in prayer!*
> *In His arms He'll take and shield thee, thou wilt find a solace there.*

Now, Jesus Christ, the very Son of the Most High God is a Friend so faithful, He is my dependable source of inner strength. He promised me His eternal companionship through His Spirit, in that I can hear Him through His word. No longer will I depend on my impulsive decisions but through the inspiration of that "still small voice" behind me saying: *"This is the way, walk in it. . ." (Isaiah 30:21).*

Motherly love made my mourning for Brian bitter and long. I took for myself the agony instead of releasing my sorrow to God, but still He understood and offered me peace. I wandered momentarily and blamed God. He did not condone my stumbling, but instead reached out to patiently guide me through the way of peace and faith. What a relief to know and have faith that my dear Brian died with a blessed hope. I was once a wandering doubting child, but now I am guided by the clear light of God's word. This was a complete turnaround from my old and empty life which had no solid foundation, except the crumbling tradition of my former church. Now I had blessed comfort from a Friend, Jesus. Now I longed for my family to share the enlightening joy that was flooding my soul. O, that my family would only take time to really consider their eternal destiny. If they could only see and avoid the path of the fools cherishing their selfish philosophy like the hopeless saying: *"Eat and be merry for tomorrow we die"* (1 Cor. 15:32). If they will only turn to God with a humble heart, God will certainly listen to give them future assurance of what shall be beyond their grave.

FIGHTING A WRONG FIGHT

Three years after I became an Adventist, in July, 2005 I attended for the first time a World General Conference in St. Louis, Missouri. Our dear son Brian was just two years gone, and my heart was still mourning. The Lord very kindly used this event to somehow extend relief and solace to my sorrowing heart. I was fascinated by the many booths with their heartwarming displays of particular ministries and give-aways. One magazine from the Share Him Global Evangelism booth caught my attention. I was deeply moved by an eight-year-old boy preacher in Africa, who participated in an evangelistic crusade resulting in the baptism of over two hundred persons. In that same magazine, there was a story of an elderly lady in a wheelchair, accompanied by her granddaughter who served as her interpreter, doing ministry for Jesus. That story made me question myself that if God could enable this old lady in spite of her disability, why couldn't God likewise provide for me a place in His vineyard? I thought about how the need for God's field workers is so great that He was utilizing even the handicapped and the very young. I knew then that I was just starting to read and understand the Bible and above all trying to find the real connection while beginning to establish my honest and right relationship with God. Nevertheless, the divine invitation to go forth was so irresistible that I felt a pure conviction to join fifty speakers and soldiers of the Lord in Morogoro, Tanzania, Africa. The enemy wanted to delay my participation by escalating further the rift in my family. He did not make it easy for me to leave for a mission trip to Africa. The devil made my daughter, Christine, become so defiant and vocal against me that she left the house and stayed with friends. But God maintained His supportive care and without coercion nor condemnation, He made provision for Christine to return home prior to my leaving for Africa.

As a new believer, I was aware that I would meet some temptations devised by the devil. Just as the Lord Jesus was Himself tempted, His followers will also be tempted and become Satan's favourite targets. But I need not be discouraged as Jesus, my Saviour, would not allow temptations that I cannot bear.

Matt and I were in constant disagreement over small things since I had come to accept Christ. Matt said that he had lost me, that I had changed in many ways, and that I had lost connections with friends. It is true that my tastes over many things changed and Matt did not understand. Of course I ceased observing Sunday masses. It was at first difficult rearranging my schedule. This was very painful for me until I came to understand fully the Sabbath of the Lord. I stopped playing *mah-jong* with my close friends. We used to go to sleep early on Friday nights and then wake up early on Saturday mornings to go to Niagara Casino.

Matt was so annoyed over my reading of the Bible before I went to sleep each night. He would not allow me to turn on any lamp, just to stop me from being able to read. I remember reading my Bible in the washroom on several occasions just so we would not fight, or else I would read before he was finished watching television.

My desire that my children and Matt be saved became more intense as I came to know more and more about Jesus. Matt at one point branded me as a *"fanatic"* as I became more obedient to the Lord. During one of our disagreements he said dejectedly, that had he known that I would become an Adventist, he would have never married me. I knew it was the devil speaking inside him. I was fighting not against my husband but the devil. Satan is so cunning that I fell into his trap to not only argue, but also sleep in a separate bed for several days.

Matt furiously challenged me in so many ways, alleging that there were many professing Adventist Christians who casually drank and gambled, just as the members of other churches were doing. I realized that our disagreements were getting nowhere. I was fighting a wrong fight.

I do not know why, but in defense of my newfound faith I turned aggressive and was easily carried into an argument as a wasteful exercise, rather than taking the high road of quietness as a confident child of God. Didn't Jesus ask us to "be wise as serpents yet be harmless as doves" (Matthew 10:16)? How easily I forgot that the battle is the Lord's. The Spirit whispered, saying to me, "Let God be God and allow Him to fight the battle for you." My greatest supplication was for God to let my imprudent husband find his way to Him.

I was getting pushed to the limit of my patience and hopelessness in trying to salvage my marriage relationship. I prayed for God to snatch my dear husband away from total hopelessness, until my Bible reading led me to the story of King David.

Although I had heard the story of this famous and popular king of Israel, to read it myself was very relieving. Somehow the Spirit of God let me see deeper into the life of this man. I came to realize from the Bible records that King David, the hero and giant killer, was also a sinner. Being the king, he had wives and concubines and had even committed illicit relations with the wife of another man. I grew curious and read further, wanting to find out what made this man "a man after God's own heart" (1 Samuel 13:14).

Ask any second or third grader who killed the nine-foot tall Goliath and his name will come out like a hero. Yes, King David, the greatest recorded King of Israel, ruled God's chosen people for a good forty years.

One of the most popular Psalms out of the seventy that he wrote is Psalm 23 that portrays God as a mighty protector, man's caregiver, and Shepherd. This Psalm even became one of the favourite readings in funeral services.

> "The Lord is my shepherd, I shall not want
> He makes me to lie in green pastures,
> He leads me beside the still waters. He restores my soul,
> He leads me in the path of righteousness for His name's sake.
> Yea, though I walk through the valley of the shadow of death,
> I will fear no evil, for you are with me,
> Your rod and your staff they comfort me.
> You prepare a table before me in the presence of my enemies,
> You anoint my head with oil, my cup runs over.
> Surely goodness and mercy shall follow me,
> all the days of my life and I will dwell in the house of the Lord forever."

King David, the great warrior, writer, and singer in his time, fell victim to the sin of adultery with Bathsheba. As a result, he was laden with enormous guilt that led him to mastermind the murder of Bathsheba's innocent and faithful husband, Uriah, who was a loyal and brave soldier in the army of King David. This was wrong and a great sin before God. His wrongdoing displeased the Lord so much that, according to the prophet of God, He caused David to place himself before a curse of having himself dishonoured by his own family. David knew the enormity of his sin and knew too well that it was punishable by death. He came to God for pardon and mercy. David realized and acknowledged his sin and repented and begged for forgiveness, and he was forgiven. He later wrote: "I acknowledged my sin to You, And my iniquity I have not hidden, I said, 'I will confess my sin to the Lord,' And You forgave the iniquity of my sin" (Psalm 32:5).

The sacred book, time and again, speaks of the long-suffering and loving God, giving sinners time to see themselves and repent. It says, *"The Lord is not slack concerning His promise, as some count slackness, but is long suffering toward us, not willing that any should perish but that all should come to repentance"* (2 Peter 3:9). And what a God we serve that in spite of our stubbornness, He is ever ready and ever willing to forgive us of our sins. God through prophet Isaiah said: *"Come now and let us reason together, says the Lord: 'Though your sins are like scarlet, they shall be as white as snow. Though they are red like crimson, they shall be as wool. If you are willing and obedient, you shall eat the good of the land. But, if you refuse and rebel, you shall be devoured by a sword. For the mouth of the Lord has spoken"* (Isaiah 1:18-20).

King David acknowledged the graciousness of God, saying: *"For You, Lord are good and ready to forgive. And abundant in mercy to all those who call upon you"* (Psalm 85:6). No other condition, except that we come to Him as one repentant soul. The God of mercy has left the door of forgiveness wide open. John the Apostle confidently said, *"If we confess our sins, He is faithful and just to forgive us our sins and to cleanse us from all unrighteousness"* (1 John 1:9).

CUBA EVANGELISM 2009

Enthusiastic church attendees singing joyfully during the opening program of the evangelistic series.

A couple committing their lives to Christ by way of baptism.

A lady emerging anew in Jesus.

Tom and I with the newly baptized as the pastor explains to the congregation the enormity of accepting Christ as Lord and Saviour without delay.

CHENNAI, INDIA EVANGELISM 2010

Myself gratefully receiving a traditional Indian welcome. I deeply appreciated how warmly the villagers embraced me.

An interpreter assists me during one of my evangelistic presentations.

Spending quality time with children and elders of the village.

Introducing the Word of God which was eagerly received by the villagers.

Leading children in Bible study.

Young people joyfully receiving Bibles, rare possessions in the village.

A captivated crowd of mostly Hindu villagers listening intently to a message about Jesus.

Guided by The Holy Spirit, an elderly Hindu woman commits her life to Christ through baptism.

Myself with the enthused group of newly baptized villagers who patiently wait to receive Bibles translated into an Indian language.

Surrounded by the beautiful children of the village.

MY UNDELIVERED LETTER TO MATT

My Dearest Husband,

God knows how much I profoundly love you.

You are the only man who owns my marriage vow, a vow which has not been diminished nor antiquated by time and age.

I will continue to uphold and preserve your name with no taint of dishonesty no matter what circumstances life brings. I have gone this far never to come off it nor to deviate from it. Yes, I loved you then, and I love you now, and you can certainly prove my love for you, even until your time comes that you will need crutches or cane for support for your ambulation. My eyes will watch you closely that you do not fall. And when your looks give way to age, given by your hair loss and teeth diminished in numbers, I will still be there.

We will fade and decline, for that is nature's cycle. Our temperaments will be erratic, and the raging tempests will happen, but by God's grace I pray that you come to His terms of handling. While there's still time, while the door of mercy remains open, settle your accounts with God, for He shall abundantly pardon. His mercy can still accommodate you. Remember the song by Ira F. Stanphill:

There's Room at the Cross for You

"Though millions have found him a friend
And have turned from the sins they have sinned
The Savior still waits to open the gates
And welcome a sinner before it's too late."

My darling, the song also says:

"Though millions have come,
There's still room for one,
Yes there's room at the cross for you."

Yes my dearest, by His grace, He gladly had one fallen like me in one of those rooms.

If and when the unpredictable parting will come to either one of us, or when that inevitable and imminent passing happens that I shall go ahead of you or you shall leave ahead of me in the Lord's own way and timing, my prayer is that neither of us shall bear the pain of despair and cry deeply for long, for the greatest hope is guaranteed to those who believe. Then when time shall be no more, in the earth made new shall they all meet again and face-to-face before the Son of God Christ Jesus, we shall all bow in reverence and gratitude for His blood that was shed on Calvary.

Soon, the greatest hope of humanity which is Christ's eminent return will become a reality. Jesus will be exalted above the proud and haughty, when "all at the name of Jesus every knee should bow, of those in heaven, and of those on earth and of those under the earth, and that every tongue should confess that Jesus Christ is Lord, to the glory of God the Father" (Philippians 2:10,11).

On that very day, I wish to see ourselves holding hands at the foot of the Lord of Lords and King of Kings, Jesus.

Loving you always,

Nora

In the year 2007, a team of ninety-five preachers were bound for Ukraine Evangelistic Tour. I was preparing to be part of this endeavour, when the confrontation between me and my husband veered from bad to worse. He became more jealous of me reading a lot of Christian books. Our bed was full of materials about the love of God, His Son, and forgiveness, for by then I was beginning to hate my husband for what he was doing.

Before I had became a Christian, I had observed my husband spending more and more worthless time outside the house. I grew angry with vengeance in my heart. I was one strong-willed person. Since coming to meet Jesus, I have asked the Lord to transform and reform my whole being.

Matt would purposely turn the television on and watch movies full of violence and crime just to provoke me to anger. He would read books about cults and witchcrafts and other literature of the same genre. He would sit next to me to make me mad or distract my concentration during my devotions. By this point Matt had stopped going to church altogether, except for Christmas. I knew the enemy was using Matt to annoy me and divert my attention from my work. I thought that I could not pursue what I was called to do if he was to distract me in our bedroom, so one night while he was out I threw all his belongings in the basement. My action implied that he could not be in the same bedroom or in the same bed with me any longer. I was certain that I could not and would never compromise my relationship with my Lord. I was hanging onto what I had come across in His Word: if we could not let go by turning our back on our family for His sake, then we are not worthy of His love.

Crying for days, I repeatedly sought Pastor Myrie's counselling. I turned to the church's prayer warriors. I had elders who supported me in my need of prayer. I fasted, for I saw the danger that was coming. There was a time I loaded myself with alcohol as I was so upset with his doings. I got drunk, so literally drunk. On one desperate occasion I thought I had suffered to the extent that I preferred death over life, and so I overdosed on my prescription for sleeping pills. I was admitted to the emergency room for overnight observation. Through this ordeal I understand what it is like to be depressed. I know how through one little mistake, a miscalculation so to speak, children are left motherless.

My relationship with my husband went from bad to worse. He blamed me, claiming that it was all my fault and the fault of the God that I now served. Matt said that the TRUE GOD does not cause separation and division in the family; therefore, I was connected to the wrong God. I was connected to a wrongful church and confused believers.

But God never left me alone. He sent an amazing child of God into my life who would play a great part in my early spiritual journey with the Lord. Mrs. Olga Lawrence of the Mississauga SDA Church will always remain very special in my heart. I turned to her for a listening ear over my pain and grief when we lost Brian. On very many occasions my pillows were soaked in tears from days of crying. On the phone, day or night, she was always there to listen to my distressed heart. She stood in the gap with her mighty and powerful prayers when my faith levels had gone under. Her words of reassurance spoke with conviction on God's undisputed promises in the Bible when I was too weak and too debilitated to speak with God. "Nora," she said, "hang in there, it will come to pass; by God's mercy and grace Matt will come around in His own calendar and time."

But Matt refused to read the Word of God, and to see the truth for himself. He bluntly refused my invitation to join me in the church service, perchance he would discover the great treasure that I had found.

How could I find comfort from these specific words of Jesus? Matthew 10:34-42, cunning (New Living Translation (NLT):

34 Don't imagine that I came to bring peace to the earth! I came not to bring peace, but a sword. 35 I have come to set a man against his father, a daughter against her mother, a daughter-in-law against her mother-in-law. 36 Your enemies will be right in your own household! 37 If you love your father or mother more than you love me, you are not worthy of being mine; or if you love your son or daughter more than me, you are not worthy of being mine. 38 If you refuse to take up your cross and follow me, you are not worthy of being mine. 39 If you cling to your life, you will lose it; but if you give up your life for me, you will find it.

40 Anyone who receives you receives me, and anyone who receives me receives the Father who sent me. 41 If you receive a prophet as one who speaks for God, you will be given the same reward as a prophet. And if you receive righteous people because of their righteousness, you will be given a reward like theirs. 42 And if you give even a cup of cold water to one of the least of my followers, you will surely be rewarded.

We didn't speak for days, and my knees became calloused from praying. I thought I had prayed enough. But I still relied on my impulse to surrender, and seek reconciliation with Tom. I would come knocking at his door in the basement and as he opened the door we would give each other a warm embrace as our act of being sorry to each other. We would be good for over a week, but the subtle enemy was very sophisticated in coming between Tom and I. We became Satan's toys; I became his prey. My friends in the church reminded me that I needed to exercise faith and trust Jesus, who had never lost a battle. I could share Jesus' victory, if I valued Jesus' love for me as being much greater than my family ties. At times like these, I should be encouraged that Jesus' words stood true and faithful. He said that He brings a sword instead of peace, and He added that *"Your enemies will be right in your own household."* I saw how truthfully this had unfolded in my very own experience. I was already on the winning side of the Master. I should have stood in faith rather than succumbed to my impulses and feelings. According to The Book of Hebrews 10:36-36: *"Therefore do not cast away your confidence which has great reward. For you have need of endurance, so that after you have done the will of God, you may receive the promise."* I claimed that promise then and still today, and although I flip in my faith so very many times, according to His awesome promise in Romans 8:28, *"We know that all things work together for good to those who love God, to those who are the called according to His purpose."* I feel I am called to do more than many others who won't, and more than many others who can't. Along with obedience and courage and His providence, He gave me the means to cross oceans and seas. He gave me the voice to be His humble speaker to those who have not yet heard about the crucified Jesus.

Many times I came to wonder about the privileges that God opened before me. Many times I wondered as to the many wasted years that God's goodness was spent in needless personal luxury. Now that He had called me to a nobler purpose, was this His way of testing my priorities? How would I show Him that love and great appreciation for His saving grace? Now I saw. I could serve my risen Saviour by sharing His goodness and saving grace to other people, who like my past, have languished in the darkness of ignorance and sin. I praised God for awakening my thoughts to something worthwhile and lasting.

Meanwhile, God has not left us alone. The Holy Spirit is here to comfort us, guide us, and transform us to live as witnesses for God's love. The same Spirit who inspired prophets and empowered Jesus, who shaped and created the world, enables and empowers each one of us. The Spirit activates the "body of Christ" - the Church - and incarnates on earth the reality and evidence of His existence.

God called His people into existence for the purpose of proclaiming what they have heard and seen and experienced in their lives, thus revealing Christ's character to the world. They are to represent Christ in all walks of life. They are redeemed for service and are made to understand that the true object of this life is to minister and serve. Whatever chosen profession a person may engage in, when that profession is dedicated for the service of Christ, He transforms their profession into a ministry as God's spiritual gift. Thus every soul becomes a minister of God's grace.

My newfound relationship with my God and Lord has widened my understanding of my humble work and profession. It has brought me to a higher level of usefulness in the hand of God as His gift to the church, when He transformed my few talents into spiritual gifts.

I have experienced various levels of spiritual joys and fulfilment ever since I consecrated my profession as a tool in the hand of God, while extending loving care to the sick and dying. I remember one experience of attending to an old Japanese lady who was dying. Despondency and despair had wasted any thread of hope in her. Sensing that she needed some ray of hope and assurance, I softly whispered:

"Do you know how sick you are?"

"Y-es, though my, er, my doctors did their er, utmost best. . ." she said, in her halting English between stifled sobs.

"Have you submitted your life to your God?" I tenderly asked her as I wiped away the tears welling from her deep sunken eyes.

Between intervals of her efforts to shake the tears away from blinding her vision, she asked me, "Who is God? I am an atheist; I do not believe there exist a God. Who is He?" she pressed.

With an effort to assure her, I said, "God created all things including us. He gave us life and He has power to take it back in His own appointed time. He so loved us, that although He will take this life of sin away, He will give us a new life where we will not get sick and we will no longer die. If we accept His offer, He will pledge an assurance of a glorious resurrection. When He comes again, He then will grant this promised eternal life to those who believe in Him."

My dying friend stopped sobbing, and she listened in spite of her pains.

I continued, "This God is here through the Spirit of His Son Jesus. He knows your suffering and he would like to introduce Himself to you. He said, *'I am the resurrection and the life, He who believes in me, though he may die, he shall live. And, whoever lives and believes in me shall never die. Do you believe this?'"* (John 11:25).

With tears in her eyes, knowing she would soon give up her last breath, she felt the most pressing news of hope for eternal life, promised by the God she had so disregarded. She felt the enormous guilt of disregarding the promptings of the Holy Spirit. As her parting breath faded, she held my hand. In her final moments, she felt the urgency to be forgiven. She found this forgiveness at the foot of a loving Savior, Jesus Christ. Weakened and wounded by the ugly thought of passing away, she sought forgiveness and found solace in the embrace of a loving God and Savior.

It was a very moving experience. I can attest to the fact that a consecrated profession, whatever it may be, can become a powerful tool in the hand of God through the ministry of compassion.

My eldest son Dexter graduated as a computer engineer from McMaster University. His energetic quickness and precision made him the Most Valuable Player and Hitter of the Year of the McMaster University Marauder's Hall of Fame in 1999. He married Cathy and the two were blessed with two adorable children: a daughter, Sydney, and a son, Max. They bought their first house in Milton, Ontario before their children were born. Dexter, Cathy, Sydney, and Max are ever present in my prayer life. In my supplication, I ask my ever-loving God to make His presence constantly abide with them. I pray that Dexter will continue to bloom as a responsible husband to Cathy and a strong father to his children and that God will continue to guard them in peace.

Our late son Brian was in the Kinesiology Program at McMaster University before we lost him.

Christine Charise, our youngest child, was gifted with a beautiful singing voice at an early age. She followed her dream of cultivating her singing talent at the Royal Conservatory of Music prior to her university studies. She finished her studies and graduated from Western University with a Bachelor of Music degree in Vocal Performance. By God's grace, Christine sings soprano. I can only ask God to tenderly bless my daughter and keep her from dangers, that her skills and voice would be a blessing to people around her; for how could a mother forget the fruit of her womb?

We were blessed with intelligent and gifted children. They are my priceless treasures. I would now be the proud mother of three gifted professionals, had not Brian died. I'm mighty proud of my two who remain on this earth, and who mean more than the world to me. In my humblest way I wish to reciprocate my God for His goodness and grace.

My solitude has been solemnly fruitful and encouraging. God's Holy Word brings me closer to Him. I feel for those who have not found the Lord and do not know Christ; they make choices as though this life were all we have. In reality, this is just the introduction to eternity. How we live this brief span, however, determines our eternal state. What we accumulate on earth has no value in purchasing eternal life. Even the highest social or civic honours cannot earn us entrance into heaven. Jesus said: *"For what profit is it to a man if he gains the whole world and loses his own soul? Or, what will a man give in exchange for his soul? For the Son of Man will come in the glory of His Father with His angels, and then He will reward each, according to his works"* (Matthew 16:26,27).

Indeed, what good are professions and titles without a functional knowledge of God? It saddens me to know people's lack of knowledge of the Way, the Truth, and the Life. It would sadden my motherly heart if my loved ones would follow the fleeting and temporal beauty of the world. As a professional nurse I wished people would avoid alcoholic drinks, for these innocent looking products can take a serious toll on one's health on a single occasion or over time. Not one organ is left unaffected from alcohol intake. Like cigarette smoking, it makes one feel good for a period of time, but it comes with devastating health effects. Little vices and innocent looking lottery games are like having pet pythons who strike and strangle their master. I hope and pray for my children to value the loving reminders of God.

This world is not our final home. We're but strangers here. God has prepared a place where His faithful children will live for eternity. Those who accepted Jesus as their Saviour are sure of a place in heaven above.

Jesus said, *"Let not your hearts be troubled. Believe in God, believe also in Me. In my Father's house are many mansions. If it were not so, I would have told you. I go to prepare a place for you, and if I go and prepare a place for you I will come again, and receive you unto Myself, that where I am, there you may be also"* (John 14:1-3). I love my children, and I long for each to develop a need for a savior. I yearn for my children to find a blessed future that will last for eternity.

There were times and moments when I thought of my very own family that I left behind during my Evangelistic Tours to faraway places. I prayed that God would send someone else who would call the attention of my dear ones for them to see Jesus, while I travelled again according to God's bidding. I cannot lay idle and wait.

I long for my very own family members' slumbering hearts to be awakened so that they understand and appreciate the path I have chosen.

Since the time I accepted Jesus as my Saviour, I have felt constrained by His love to share my knowledge of Him. The Lord has given me a love to seek after people who are languishing in spiritual darkness. This is the reason I got hooked with the Share Him Ministries. When there are appeals and a pressing need for missionary volunteers, I want to serve. Jesus Christ, the Lord of the Harvest, said, *". . .The harvest truly is plentiful but the labourers are few. Therefore, pray to the Lord of the harvest to send out labourers into His harvest"* (Matthew 9:37-38).

Looking back and considering the enormous distance occupied by my spiritual journey, I felt that the real battle had just begun. My participation in God's foreign missions could not appease nor ease the enormity of pain on my back for carrying my personal domestic load. The battle seemed to grow more fierce and tedious, what with having a spiritually misguided husband and children who mistook my love for hatred. I asked myself, why I was going so far from home when I had a battle to fight at my home front?

A mother and a missionary author, Ellen White, in her book entitled *Christian Service* posed a challenge to all parents and workers with regard to the upbringing of their children, saying: *"The home is the child's first school, and it is here that the foundation should be laid for a life of service. The first great business of your life is to be a missionary at home"* (Christian Service, p. 206.2). The author continues: *"The restoration and uplifting of humanity begins in the home . . . our work for Christ begins with the family. . . Let not parents forget the great mission field that lies before them in the home. . . There is no missionary field more important than this"* (Ibid, 206.6).

Was I focusing my vision on a far distant field? Certainly God can make my services valuable wherever they are needed. But if I was gladdened by the conversion of people from faraway lands, would not my joy be doubly enormous when my own children turned their hearts to the God I passionately serve? My vision needed refocusing. I believed that God by His grace had given me better tools and more understanding skills after some years of experience. My church offered instruction and strategies concerning fighting the battle in my own front yard. Paul disclosed his strategy thus: *"We are humans, but we don't wage war with human plans and* methods. *We use God's mighty weapons not merely worldly methods to knock down the devil's strongholds. With these weapons we break down every proud argument that keeps people from knowing God. [Rather] with these weapons we conquer their rebellious ideas and we teach them to obey Christ" (2Corinthians 10:3-5 TLB)*. Then Paul contrasted God's method against our faulty method, saying, *"The trouble with you, is that you make your decisions on the basis of appearance" (vs. 7TLB)*.

The Scripture is replete with God's reminder to fight the battle of faith. He said through prophet Zechariah: *"It is not by force nor by strength, but by my Spirit, says the Lord Almighty" (Zech. 4:6)*. Now, I could see that the real battle that I had to fight was within me. I thank God for patiently working on me. May my God use this humble vessel of His wonderful grace for the benefit of people who are blinded by spiritual darkness.

MY LAMP BEGINS TO SHINE

My forty years of religious darkness and ignorance finally gave way to an amazing power: the Spirit of truth. This truth that came from God's Holy Word is the very foundation the remnant people of God hold. I realized that upon the gentle wooing of the Holy Spirit, I was gently accepting the Bible as the solid source and basis upon which my beliefs were gladly forming. I joined the throng of people whom I now consider my own brothers and sisters in Christ. We believe our movement to be the result of the Protestant conviction *Sola Scriptura* - the Bible as the only standard of faith and practice for Christians. Currently, I am advancing with great joy as new truths and spiritual enlightenments fill my soul. These enlightenments are fundamental to my faith about the doctrines of God, man, salvation, the church, the Christian life, and last day events. In each teaching, God is the architect Who in wisdom, grace, and infinite love is restoring a relationship with humanity that will last for eternity.

I now joyfully embrace what the Bible says about God. I used to wonder who God is. What are His claims upon my life, that I should devote time and attention to Him? WHO IS GOD? In the pages ahead I would like to share with you, my readers, the source of my strength and comfort, and the fundamentals of my newfound faith. Through these truths I found the meaning of my life and reason for my existence.

The Only True God

My darkness about God the Father is almost over now. The following titles of supremacy belong alone to Him Who is from everlasting to everlasting, the only wise God.

"The Eternal God" Deut. 33:27
"Whose Name Alone is Jehovah" Ps.83:18
"The Most High God" Mark 5:7
"The Ancient of Days" Dan. 7:13
"God Alone" Ps. 86:10
"Lord Alone" Neh. 9:6
"God of Heaven" Dan. 2:44
"The Only True God" John 17:8
"Who Only hath Immortality" 1 Tim. 6:16
"The King Eternal, Immortal, Invisible" 1 Tim. 1:17
"The Only Wise God" 1 Tim.1:17
"Lord God Omnipotent" Rev.19:6
"The Blessed and only Potentate" 1 Tim. 6:15
"Besides Me there is no God" Isa. 44:6
"God the Father" 1 Cor. 8:6
"The God of our Lord Jesus Christ, the Father of Glory" Eph. 1:17
"God and Father of all, who is above all" Eph. 4:6
"The Almighty God" Gen. 17:1
"I Am that I Am" Ex. 3:14
"Lord God Almighty" Rev. 4:8

God the Father is love, power, and splendour. His ways are far beyond us, but He still reaches out to us. God is infinite yet intimate, all-knowing yet all-forgiving. We will spend eternity cherishing an ever-deepening relationship with God the Father, with His Begotten Son Christ Jesus, and with the Holy Spirit, The Spirit of God. God is all-powerful and all-loving; God truly loves us, yet this love can only be comprehended by understanding that God gave His only begotten son Jesus Christ.

It is a cardinal fact that when the word "God" is used in its absolute sense, to denote "the most high God", "the Sovereign of the universe", or "the only true God", then there is only one God: God, the Father, beside which there is no God.

The Bible teaches that there is only one God. Both the Old and New Testaments teach this essential fact. *God is immortal, all-powerful, all-knowing, above all, and ever present. He is infinite and beyond human comprehension, yet known through His self-revelation. God, who is love, is forever worthy of worship, adoration, and service by the whole creation* (Gen. 1:26; Deut. 6:4; Isa. 6:8; Matt. 28:19; John 3:16 2 Cor. 1:21, 22; 13:14; Eph. 4:4-6; 1 Peter 1:2).

Despite the distance sin demands, God has revealed Himself in countless ways. The Bible is the story of God striving to reconnect with His children, and this is the powerful instrument God uses to reach us. A mosaic of authors, styles, and perspectives, the Bible reveals a God who is ever-creative, ever-patient, and ever-seeking to restore our relationship with Him. Though written by ordinary people, through the Holy Spirit the Bible pierces our hearts, opens our eyes, and convinces us to live for Him.

God the Father reached out to us most dramatically through His begotten Son Jesus, who chose not to just visit us, but to become one of us. Born human so we could be reborn in the Spirit, Jesus showed us His Father's love and character - and how far God the Father was willing to send His Son into the world to save us from self-destruction. What we could not do for ourselves, Jesus Christ did for us, paying the price for our sins, and dying in our place so we can live forever. He conquered death through resurrection, and promised to return to take us home.

To the four corners of the habitable globe, Christ declared God's love to the human race, His Father's love leading His mission to a lost world.

John 3:16: "For God so loved the world that He gave His only begotten Son, that whoever believes in Him should not perish but have everlasting life."

The Son of God is "the begotten", "the upheld", "the exalted", and "the glorified" BY THE FATHER.

Declarations concerning the Son of God:

> "He is the beginning of the creation of God" Rev. 3:14
> "The firstborn of every creature" Col.1:15
> "The only begotten of the Father" John 1:18; 3:18
> "The Son of the Living God" Matt.16:16
> "Existed before he came into the world" John 5:58; Micah 5:2; John 17:5
> "Was made higher than the angels" Heb. 1:14
> "He made the world and all things" John 1:1-3; Eph. 3;3, 9
> "He is the resurrection and the life" John 11:25
> "He is the appointed heir of all things" Heb.1-2
> "The head of Christ is God" 1 Cor. 11:3
> "Jesus says he could do nothing of himself" John 5:19
> "That he came not to do his own will, but the will of him that sent him" John 6:38
> "That the Father which sent him, gave him a commandment what he should say and what he should speak" John 12:49
> "And that his doctrine was not his, but the Father's which sent him" John 7:16; 12:49; 14:10, 24

God has not left us alone. The Holy Spirit of the Father is here to comfort us, guide us, and transform us to live as witnesses for God's love. The same Spirit who inspired prophets and empowered Jesus, who shaped The Holy Scripture and created the world, enables and empowers each one of us. The Holy Spirit activates the "body of Christ" - the church - through spiritual gifts and a humble attitude of service and compassion.

GOD'S HOLY WORD

I used to look at the Bible as a book to shun and avoid until I saw someone who cherished Bible reading as part of her lifestyle. What kind of book is this book they call the Holy Scriptures? I can only summarize my thoughts about this book as it has been regarded by many saints of God.

The Bible, God's Holy Book, is ancient and timeless, and is considered a masterpiece of literature. It reveals God's role in human history, it shows our place in God's plan, and it serves as the truth to guide us and shield us from deception.

The Holy Scriptures, both Old and New Testaments, are the written Word of God, given by divine inspiration. The inspired authors spoke and wrote as they were moved by the Holy Spirit. In this Word, God has committed to humanity the knowledge necessary for salvation. The Holy Scriptures are the supreme, the authoritative, and the infallible revelation of His will. They are the standard of character, the test of experience, the definitive revealer of doctrines, and the trustworthy record of God's acts in history (Ps. 119:105; Prov. 30:5, 6; Isa. 8:20; John 17:17; 1 Thess. 2:13; 2 Tim. 3:16, 17; Heb. 4:12; 2 Peter 1:20, 21).

BROKEN BEAUTY

I was among the many who question God's loving intentions to mankind because of the many evils that I could see around me. If God made his beautiful creation from the beginning, where did all this evil and rottenness come from? God's Holy Scriptures are not keeping any secrets. He created a beautiful creation, but when sin entered, God's creation was marred and rendered a broken beauty.

From neurons to nebulae, DNA to distant galaxies, we are surrounded by wonder. Yet the beauty is broken.

Genesis tells us that a loving God split light from darkness and land from water, setting life in motion and sculpting the first human from clay. Genesis describes God's joy and satisfaction in His work, again and again delighting that each new feature is "good". Earth flourished in perfect harmony, cared for by humanity.

God celebrated His work by declaring a weekly holiday, the Sabbath, a day to remember our connection with our Creator. God designed humanity to reflect His glory, each of us echoing a unique facet of His personality and character. Mind, body, and spirit, we think, live, and meditate. The astounding component?

We owe our very breath to God, yet He gave us freedom to choose - a trait that risks catastrophe. A clever lie caused the first humans to question God's love and trustworthiness. Soon fear, envy, and indifference scarred the world. Separating us from God, sin warped all that was good. Hearts rebelled. Bodies decayed. Relationships rotted. We could not reach God on our own; God would have to come to us. And so God did, sending His Son to rebuild the shattered relationship between heaven and earth. God sent His Spirit to mend the disfigured image of God in us. The Holy Spirit empowers us to reach out to others, demonstrating love and representing our Saviour and Creator to a broken world we're called to repair.

God made our world with brilliant creativity and tender care. He created humanity to take care of and take pleasure in the planet, with rest and recreation in perfect balance.

God has revealed in Scripture the authentic and historical account of His creative activity. He created the universe, and in a recent six-day creation the Lord made "the heavens and the earth, the sea, and all that is in them", and then He rested on the seventh day. Thus He established the Sabbath as a perpetual memorial of the work He performed and completed during six literal days that together with the Sabbath constituted the same unit of time that we call a week today. The first man and woman were made in the image of God as the crowning work of Creation, given dominion over the world, and charged with responsibility to care for it. When the world was finished it was "very good", declaring the glory of God (Gen. 1-2; 5; 11; Exod. 20:8-11; Ps. 19:1–6; 33:6, 9; 104; Isa. 45:12, 18; Acts 17:24; Col. 1:16; Heb. 1:2; 11:3; Rev. 10:6; 14:7).

Once moulded in God's image, now fractured by sin, it took a perfect Savior to reconcile us. The Holy Spirit restores God's reflection within us so God can work through us.

THE NATURE OF MAN

Man and woman were made in the image of God with individuality: the power and freedom to think and to do. Though created free beings, each is an indivisible unity of body, mind, and spirit, dependent upon God for life and breath and all else. When our first parents disobeyed God, they denied their dependence upon Him and fell from their high position. The image of God in them was marred and they became subject to death. Their descendants share this fallen nature and its consequences. They are born with weaknesses and tendencies to evil. But God in Christ reconciled the world to Himself and by His Spirit restores in penitent mortals the image of their Maker. Created for the glory of God, they are called to love Him and one another, and to care for their environment (Gen. 1:26-28; 2:7, 15; 3; Ps. 8:4-8; 51:5, 10; 58:3; Jer. 17:9; Acts 17:24-28; Rom. 5:12-17; 2 Cor. 5:19, 20; Eph. 2:3; 1 Thess. 5:23; 1 John 3:4; 4:7, 8, 11, 20).

THE GREAT CONTROVERSY (ORIGIN OF SIN)

Satan accused God of being untrustworthy and unfair. God gave us freedom to choose, and human history shows the result of rebellion - and the incredible power of God's love to save us. All humanity is now involved in a great controversy between Christ and Satan regarding the character of God, His law, and His sovereignty over the universe. This conflict originated in heaven when a created being, endowed with freedom of choice, in self-exaltation became Satan, God's adversary, and led into rebellion a portion of the angels. He introduced the spirit of rebellion into this world when he led Adam and Eve into sin. This human sin resulted in the distortion of the image of God in humanity, the disordering of the created world, and its eventual devastation at the time of the global flood, as presented in the historical account of Genesis 1-11. Observed by the whole creation, this world became the arena of the universal conflict out of which the God of love will ultimately be vindicated. To assist His people in this controversy, Christ sent the Holy Spirit and the loyal angels to guide, protect, and sustain them in the way of salvation (Gen. 3; 6-8; Job 1:6-12; Isa. 14:12-14; Ezek. 28:12-18; Rom. 1:19-32; 3:4; 5:12-21; 8:19-22; 1 Cor. 4:9; Heb. 1:14; 1 Peter 5:8; 2 Peter 3:6; Rev. 12:4-9).

THE LIFE, DEATH, AND RESURRECTION OF JESUS CHRIST

God sent Jesus, His only begotten Son, to live the perfect life for us, so we could not die the death our sins deserve. When we accept Jesus' sacrifice, we claim eternal life.

In Christ's life of perfect obedience to God's will, His suffering, death, and resurrection, God provided the only means of atonement for human sin, so that those who by faith accept this atonement may have eternal life, and the whole creation may better understand the infinite and holy love of the Creator. This perfect atonement vindicates the righteousness of God's law and the graciousness of His character, for it both condemns our sin and provides for our forgiveness. The death of Christ is substitutionary and expiatory, reconciling and transforming. The bodily resurrection of Christ proclaims God's triumph over the forces of evil, and for those who accept the atonement assures their final victory over sin and death. It declares the Lordship of Jesus Christ, before whom every knee in heaven and on earth will bow (Gen. 3:15; Ps. 22:1; Isa. 53; John 3:16; 14:30; Rom. 1:4; 3:25; 4:25; 8:3, 4; 1 Cor. 15:3, 4, 20-22; 2 Cor. 5:14, 15, 19-21; Phil. 2:6-11; Col. 2:15; 1 Peter 2:21, 22; 1 John 2:2; 4:10).

MY EXPERIENCE OF SALVATION

Jesus said that the Holy Spirit "proceedeth from the Father" (John 15:26). The Holy Spirit is the Spirit of the Father, and He sends His Spirit to us through His Son Jesus Christ. When we receive the gift of the Holy Spirit, we receive both the Spirit of the Father and the Spirit of Christ. (Romans 8:9-11)

When I finally accepted God's grace and salvation, the Holy Spirit revealed my need for Jesus and recreated His character in me. Christ began His work by patiently building my faith and helping me leave my broken life behind.

In God's infinite love and mercy, He made Christ, His sinless Son, who knew no sin, to be sin for me, so that in Him I might appear righteous before God. Led by the Holy Spirit we sense our need, acknowledge our sinfulness, repent of our transgressions, and exercise faith in Jesus as Saviour and Lord, Substitute, and Example. This saving faith comes through the divine power of the Word and is the gift of God's grace. Through Christ we are justified, adopted as God's sons and daughters, and delivered from the lordship of sin.

Through the Holy Spirit we are born again and sanctified. The Holy Spirit renews our minds, writes God's law of love in our hearts, and gives us the power to live a holy life. Abiding in Him we become partakers of the divine nature and have the assurance of salvation now and in the judgment (Gen. 3:15; Isa. 45:22; 53; Jer. 31:31-34; Ezek. 33:11; 36:25-27; Hab. 2:4; Mark 9:23, 24; John 3:3-8, 16; 16:8; Rom. 3:21-26; 8:1-4, 14-17; 5:6-10; 10:17; 12:2; 2 Cor. 5:17-21; Gal. 1:4; 3:13, 14, 26; 4:4-7; Eph. 2:4-10; Col. 1:13, 14; Titus 3:3-7; Heb. 8:7-12; 1 Peter 1:23; 2:21, 22; 2 Peter 1:3, 4; Rev. 13:8).

GROWING IN CHRIST

Experiencing salvation transforms how we see our world. We no longer fear our pasts or future, but embrace a present full of hope, love, passion, and praise as the Holy Spirit lives in us.

By His death on the cross Jesus triumphed over the forces of evil. He who subjugated the demonic spirits during His earthly ministry has broken their power and made certain their ultimate doom. Jesus' victory gives us victory over the evil forces that still seek to control us, as we walk with Him in peace, joy, and assurance of His love. Now the Holy Spirit dwells within us and empowers us. Continually committed to Jesus as our Saviour and Lord, we are set free from the burden of our past deeds. No longer do we live in the darkness, fear of evil powers, ignorance, and meaninglessness of our former way of life. In this new freedom in Jesus, we are called to grow into the likeness of His character, communing with Him daily in prayer, feeding on His Word, meditating on it and on His providence, singing His praises, gathering together for worship, and participating in the mission of the Church. We are also called to follow Christ's example by compassionately ministering to the physical, mental, social, emotional, and spiritual needs of humanity. As we give ourselves in loving service to those around us and in witnessing to His salvation, His constant presence with us through the Holy Spirit transforms every moment and every task into a spiritual experience (1 Chron. 29:11; Ps. 1:1, 2; 23:4; 77:11, 12; Matt. 20:25-28; 25:31-46; Luke 10:17-20; John 20:21; Rom. 8:38, 39; 2 Cor. 3:17, 18; Gal. 5:22-25; Eph. 5:19, 20; 6:12-18; Phil. 3:7-14; Col. 1:13, 14; 2:6, 14, 15; 1 Thess. 5:16-18, 23; Heb. 10:25; James 1:27; 2 Peter 2:9; 3:18; 1 John 4:4).

BAPTISM

Baptism symbolizes and declares our new faith in Christ and our trust in His forgiveness. Buried in the water, we arise to a new life in Jesus, empowered by the Holy Spirit.

By baptism we confess our faith in the death and resurrection of Jesus Christ, and testify of our death to sin and of our purpose to walk in newness of life. Thus we acknowledge Christ as Lord and Saviour, become His people, and are received as members by His church. Baptism is a symbol of our union with Christ, the forgiveness of our sins, and our reception of the Holy Spirit. We receive the Holy Spirit by immersion in water, contingent on an affirmation of faith in Jesus, and evidence of repentance of sin. Baptism follows instruction in the Holy Scriptures and conveys acceptance of their teachings (Matt. 28:19, 20; Acts 2:38; 16:30-33; 22:16; Rom. 6:1-6; Gal. 3:27; Col. 2:12, 13).

GOD'S LAW

Do you know that God has given us power to obey?

The Ten Commandments reveal God's will and love for us. Its guidelines tell how to relate to God and others. Jesus lived out the law as both our example and perfect substitute.

The great principles of God's law are embodied in the Ten Commandments and exemplified in the life of Christ. They express God's love, will, and purposes concerning human conduct and relationships and are binding upon all people in every age. These precepts are the basis of God's covenant with His people and the standard in God's judgment. The Holy Spirit points out sin and awakens a sense of need of a Saviour. Salvation is all of grace and not of works, and its fruit is obedience to the Commandments. This obedience develops Christian character and results in a sense of well-being. Our obedience is evidence of our love for the Lord and our concern for our fellow human beings. The obedience of faith demonstrates the power of Christ to transform lives, and therefore strengthen Christian witness

(Exod. 20:1-17; Deut. 28:1-14; Ps. 19:7-14; 40:7, 8; Matt. 5:17-20; 22:36-40; John 14:15; 15:7-10; Rom. 8:3, 4; Eph. 2:8-10; Heb. 8:8-10; 1 John 2:3; 5:3; Rev. 12:17; 14:12).

THE SEVENTH-DAY SABBATH

Do you know that God gives us a specific twenty-four hour period each week to rest, reflect on Him, and spend time with our families?

The Sabbath is God's gift to us, a time for rest and restoration of our connection to God and others. It reminds us of God's creation and Jesus' grace.

The gracious Creator, after the six days of Creation, rested on the seventh day and instituted the Sabbath for all people as a memorial of Creation. The fourth commandment of God's unchangeable law requires the observance of this seventh-day Sabbath as the day of rest, worship, and ministry in harmony with the teaching and practice of Jesus, the Lord of the Sabbath. The Sabbath is a day of delightful communion with God and one another. It is a symbol of our redemption in Christ, a sign of our sanctification, a token of our allegiance, and a foretaste of our eternal future in God's kingdom. The Sabbath is God's perpetual sign of His eternal covenant between Him and His people. Joyful observance of this holy time from evening to evening, sunset to sunset, is a celebration of God's creative and redemptive acts (Gen. 2:1-3; Exod. 20:8-11; 31:13-17; Lev. 23:32; Deut. 5:12-15; Isa. 56:5, 6; 58:13, 14; Ezek. 20:12, 20; Matt. 12:1-12; Mark 1:32; Luke 4:16; Heb. 4:1-11).

THE LORD'S SUPPER

Do you know there is a celebration that expresses our closeness to Christ and willingness to serve others?

The Lord's Supper symbolizes our acceptance of the body and blood of Jesus, spilled and broken for us. By searching our hearts and washing one another's feet, we remember Jesus' humble example of service.

The Lord's Supper is a participation in the emblems of the body and blood of Jesus as an expression of faith in Him, our Lord and Saviour. In this experience of communion Christ is present to meet and strengthen His people. As we partake, we joyfully proclaim the Lord's death until He comes again. Preparation for the Supper includes self-examination, repentance, and confession. The Master ordained the service of foot-washing to signify renewed cleansing, to express a willingness to serve one another in Christ-like humility, and to unite our hearts in love. The communion service is open to all believing Christians (Matt. 26:17-30; John 6:48-63; 13:1-17; 1 Cor. 10:16, 17; 11:23-30; Rev. 3:20).

THE SECOND COMING OF CHRIST

We look forward to Jesus' promised return, when He will resurrect His saved children and take them to heaven. Though we cannot know exactly when He will come back, we can live in joyful anticipation.

The second coming of Christ is the blessed hope of the church, the grand climax of the gospel. The Saviour's coming will be literal, personal, visible, and worldwide. When He returns, the righteous dead will be resurrected, and together with the righteous living will be glorified and taken to heaven, but the unrighteous will die. The almost complete fulfillment of most lines of prophecy, together with the present condition of the world, indicate that Christ's coming is near. The time of that event has not been revealed, and we are therefore exhorted to be ready at all times (Matt. 24; Mark 13; Luke 21; John 14:1-3; Acts 1:9-11; 1 Cor. 15:51-54; 1 Thess. 4:13-18; 5:1-6; 2 Thess. 1:7-10; 2:8; 2 Tim. 3:1-5; Titus 2:13; Heb. 9:28; Rev. 1:7; 14:14-20; 19:11-21).

MARRIAGE AND FAMILY

Created in God's image, male and female, we are designed to live in relationships. Marriage is God's ideal to live in harmony, and for children to grow up in security and love.

Marriage was divinely established in Eden and affirmed by Jesus to be a lifelong union between a man and a woman in loving companionship. For the Christian a marriage commitment is to God as well as to the spouse, and should be entered into only by a man and a woman who share a common faith. Mutual love, honour, respect, and responsibility are the fabric of this relationship, which is to reflect the love, sanctity, closeness, and permanence of the relationship between Christ and His church. Regarding divorce, Jesus taught that the person who divorces a spouse, except for fornication, and marries another, commits adultery. Although some family relationships may fall short of the ideal, a man and a woman who fully commit themselves to each other in Christ through marriage may achieve loving unity through the guidance of the Holy Spirit and the nurturing of the church. God blesses the family and intends that its members shall assist each other toward complete maturity. Increasing family closeness is one of the earmarks of the final gospel message. Parents are to bring up their children to love and obey the Lord. By their example and their words parents are to teach their children that Christ is a loving, tender, and caring guide who wants them to become members of His body, the family of God which embraces both single and married persons (Gen. 2:18-25; Exod. 20:12; Deut. 6:5-9; Prov. 22:6; Mal. 4:5, 6; Matt. 5:31, 32; 19:3-9, 12; Mark 10:11, 12; John 2:1-11; 1 Cor. 7:7, 10, 11; 2 Cor. 6:14; Eph. 5:21-33; 6:1-4).

I can only write this synopsis of the great discoveries of my life because the Lord Jesus graciously found me. I am thrilled to constantly grow in my spiritual experience. It's a joy to be part of the worldwide church family, who rightly represent the remnant people of God in these last days embracing the challenge of announcing the Second Advent of Christ.

SHARE HIM INTERNATIONAL: GLOBAL EVANGELISM EXPERIENCE

Share Him International is a ministry of the Carolina Conference of the Seventh-day Adventist Church, whose ultimate goal is to empower and mobilize laymen and laywomen to be active in a lifestyle of evangelism. Share Him International has two campaign categories: International Campaign and Homeland Initiative.

The international campaigns are for people, mainly laymen, from economically developed countries to go and be inspired in parts of the world where the message is spreading fast, like Africa, Central America etc. by preaching a series of evangelistic meetings.

The homeland initiative is targeted at churches in developed countries who want to start a continuous cycle of evangelism-living, called *evangeliving*. This initiative involves both sowing (continuous mission activities in the church) and reaping events. These goals are achieved through local conferences.

It has been my humble privilege to be part of this endeavour through the international campaigns. This was a hectic and very rewarding experience for me, considering I was very new to the faith. With much supplication, the Lord paved the way for my participation as one of His volunteer field workers. In this case we were called God's Commissioners responding to the gospel commission of Jesus:

"Go ye therefore and make disciples of all nations, baptizing them in the name of the Father, and of the Son and of the Holy Spirit. Teaching them to observe all things, whatsoever I have commanded you, and lo, I am with you always, even to the end of the age" (Matthew 28:19, 20).

God made it possible for me to be one of His fieldworkers, believing that *"this Gospel of the kingdom will be preached in all the world as a witness to all the nations and then the end will come" (Matthew 24: 14).*

TANZANIA, AFRICA - 2005

My first International venture with *Share Him* took place in Tanzania, in an East African country known for its Mount Kilimanjaro - the highest mountain in Africa. We were fifty volunteer speakers of varied races and backgrounds from different countries. We were teachers, pastors, students, nurses, a lawyer, plain housewives, an engineer, an accountant, and retirees of various working backgrounds. An engineer came with his wife and their ten-year-old son who was also assigned to be a speaker alternating with his father. There were several university students from Germany who also joined our group. We were all unified by our one and only objective - to win people to Christ.

We were warmly welcomed by church pastors and church leaders with a wonderful dinner. Our all-day long general orientation included a briefing about the people's cultural background and getting to know our interpreter who would help us speakers to efficiently deliver the messages for the event. It was a very interesting warm up session, especially for me being a new speaker.

We all boarded a charter bus that drove us to our respective lodgings. One elderly male captivated my heart just before he got off the charter bus. He took off his hat and then said to everyone in his calm, clear voice: "'Til we meet again on the resurrection morning," to which everyone joyously responded, "'Til we meet again, brother." What a wonderful exchange of affirmation and faith for the blessed promise of the Lord, to all His believers: the assurance of seeing each other again on the blessed resurrection. I said to myself, "They must truly know the Shepherd and LORD Whom I have just found not too long ago, and Whom I am just getting to know myself."

My team was assigned lodging in a small motel where we would have ample time for solitude. I experienced spiritual refreshment and growth in the grace and knowledge of my Lord and Saviour, Jesus Christ. I learned to supplicate not only on behalf of myself but for the rest of the group as well. I learned to have an intense and intimate solitude with the Lord that He would give me the grace and anoint my lips every day as I spoke.

Out of fifty speakers scattered over different parts of Tanzania, five of us were assigned to the town of Morogoro. Our group was composed of one elementary school teacher from Johannesburg, South Africa; a medical student from California; a pastor from Chicago; Marianne, a medical scientist from North Carolina, USA; and myself, a Registered Nurse from Mississauga, Ontario, Canada.

As a nurse I have taken care of patients with full-blown malaria, and malaria is what I feared the most as I prepared for my flight to Tanzania. Malaria is a highly infectious and prevalent disease from mosquito bites. In fact, it is a life-threatening disease. I was elated when I was sent to Morogoro University instead of being assigned to a group whose meeting places were on open fields. God surely knew my vulnerabilities, being young in the faith, and so He saw to it that I wouldn't become discouraged. All of my own team sessions were held in the early evenings at the campus gymnasium. The students were very enthused, and they tried their best not to miss any sessions of the series.

The phonetics of the Swahili language of Tanzania were very interesting to me, and within a couple of days I was able to read clearly the Swahili Translated Bible before the throng. I must have impressed the people, because they applauded vigorously and showed renewed enthusiasm in their interactions and response.

For the three weeks' duration of the Evangelism series, two capable translators took turns: an accounting instructor from the university, and a high school teacher. Our lodgings were in walking distance to a small restaurant that became our favourite place for lunch and very late dinners after our nightly meetings.

The people were pathetically poor and yet warm. Surprisingly not one of us saw any policeman manning the streets during the whole three weeks of our stay in that town. People say that no lawbreaker would ever make it to the police station, as they would be handled by the people themselves. Our small team made sure that we met to share any updates before we rested for the night, and most importantly, we got down on our knees each evening, implicitly pleading for the Holy Spirit to make us His effective speakers in Jesus' blessed name. We prayed that people would come to understand their dire need of Christ so that they perish not. We never missed asking the Lord for our utmost safety, because the enemy and his troops were actively watching and plotting to derail God's work.

There was jubilation in my team when twenty-nine people, aided by God's loving Spirit, responded to the call and accepted Christ as their Lord and Saviour. We ascribed to God the glory and honour for the things He has done.

KIEV, UKRAINE - SEPTEMBER 2007

There was a time during the 1990s in Ukraine that if someone had a Bible in his hand to give away, about a hundred people would run for it. That was how scarce the Holy Book was then. The people were hungering and thirsting for God's presence under the communist regime. Most if not all were praying and clamouring for their national independence, until this was finally granted. Many things have changed since then.

The team of ninety-five Share Him lay evangelists were spread throughout Kiev. The atmosphere in Kiev differed from that of the third world. From the efforts of ninety-five preachers who laboured for the Gospel Truth, a measly total of ten souls were harvested. According to the story of believers, in Romania, several years prior to Kiev Evangelism, out of fifty who preached the word of God, not one responded to the call for baptism. But we were there to plant the seeds, and we did not know when they would grow and sprout. We were not discouraged. Ecclesiastes 11:6 says, *"In the morning sow your seed, and in the evening do not withhold your hand; for you do not know which one will prosper. Either this or that, or, whether both alike will be good."*

My group presented only one precious soul for the kingdom - precious because Jesus was also for such a one as him .

CUBA - 2009

My opening night started out with me before a church that was almost completely filled with people. Attendance grew each night until there were no longer any seats available, and so many had to remain standing until the service was over. The attendance situation remained almost unchanged during the whole duration of the evangelistic series. I preached my favourite opening night message: The Returning Judge.

It was an answered prayer that Matt joined me in Cuba. My nightly presentation had already been running for a week when he arrived. I was ever grateful to the Lord that He allowed my husband to hear me speak with passion and conviction of the great love of the Almighty Father to man. A stirring and heart-warming song written by Frederick M. Lehman in 1917 illustrates the love of God:

> *The love of God is greater far*
> *Than tongue or pen can ever tell;*
> *It goes beyond the highest star,*
> *And reaches to the lowest hell;.....*
> *Oh, love of God how rich and pure!*
> *How measureless and strong!......*
> *To write the love of God above*
> *Would drain the Ocean dry;*
> *Nor could the scroll contain the whole,*
> *Though stretched from sky to sky.*

About forty years ago in Cuba, the government banned the distribution of Bibles. The records now show that Christianity is growing rapidly in Cuba and there are a few Bibles around for sale, but then again, many people could not afford to buy a Bible even if there was one available. That year that I went to Cuba, out of a congregation of no less than one hundred and fifty, only three or four owned Bibles.

A certain event touched me one evening when I announced that I had some little gifts for them. Yes, people patiently lined up for just a couple of rubber bands, a third of a pencil, and an inch-sized eraser which had been cut into three just so every person would receive one.

Throughout the campaign, I was helped by a young and energetic seventeen-year-old male Spanish student interpreter. From day one I began announcing the topic for the last meeting, explaining that it would be about a place called "*Heaven*", a real place where there will be no more pain, sorrow, or death. I told them enthusiastically not to miss it.

Amazingly, by the last night we had a fully packed church. Some people had even been picked up by special transport vehicles from neighbouring towns. The excitement on the faces of everyone was a joy to behold. The church became like a concert hall with beautiful Spanish singing by sopranos and altos and the breathtaking accompaniment from an accordion played by the pastor's young son.

By the end of the three-week series, there were seventeen repentant and overjoyed hearts who had accepted Jesus, the Way, the Truth, and the Life. Seventeen souls publicly professed their repentance and faith in Jesus and they went through the baptism water by immersion. It was a blessing for me to witness two deliriously happy couples who could not seem to contain their joy, giving each other a hug and a kiss just as they got into the watery pool. I was purely delighted myself, and as I joined the clapping of hands in the jubilant crowd, I said to myself, "What a great honour and humbling experience it has been for me indeed, to be one of those who embraced the call of The Master to help out in His vineyard."

The last day of goodbye has always been the hardest for me. With my saddened heart I said that there is an appointed time when we will meet each other again by God's grace. When the divine trumpet sounds on that marvelous resurrection morning, we'll meet again, never more to part, provided we remain ever faithful and obedient to the will of God.

CHENNAI, INDIA - DECEMBER 2010

We were fourteen highly spirited fieldworkers of Christ who went to Chennai, each one with the same passion to reach, teach, and preach about Calvary's Cross, the undeniable nearness of the end of the earth's history, and many other pre-arranged topics.

We were all housed in a small hotel with individual transportation provided. Trips from the hotel to our village were assigned in advance for our own security and that of our translators, and to ensure that each one of us arrived at our place of work on time. The trip to the small village where I was assigned was a two-hour drive. The crowded and poorly lit streets of human traffic made our nightly trip so slow. I was in constant prayer that we would not hit anyone along the busy, dark, and crowded road.

This village was considered one of the most overly populated and underprivileged, where 87% of the people identified themselves as Hindus. The rest of the population adhered to Islam, Sikhism, Buddhism, Jainism, and other religions, including only a pathetically small percentage of Christians.

The Hindu villagers had no idea about the most unforgettable and cruelest global event: the day mankind was purchased for a price by the blood of Christ. The villagers had never heard of the Plan of Salvation that the Father and His begotten Son made available for each one of them, that whosoever believes will be saved, young and old, whatsoever condition they are in.

We were carefully warned and repeatedly cautioned regarding the notoriety of the place. Nevertheless, the power of God Who makes no mistake was fully manifested all throughout our evangelistic campaign. He safeguarded all of us from the threatening hands of the hardcore and extremely explicit Hindu village leaders. Unseen divine hands absolutely guarded our team of five people including myself, and feeling certain, we walked around the small village from one house to another to extend our personal invitation to residents who may wish to attend the nightly event. I felt saddened by people's reactions in the severely poverty-stricken village. The majority of those we came in contact with would shy away whenever we talked to them, but my little hug and handshake made them feel special, and they showed up at the meeting. My heart was strained by the living conditions of the more impoverished villagers who were only able to come up with the smallest amounts of food to eat. Due to great poverty, I was told that some could only eat every other day.

The whole team met early each morning for updates and corporate prayers in addition to our respective private prayers. We depended on prayer as our ultimate weapon and assurance of God's protection upon His fieldworkers. Yes, we pleaded every morning collectively and individually for the Lord to guide our lips that our messages be received, perceived, and accepted by most if not by all.

With my interpreter's help, the message of salvation was heard. I announced that suffering from hunger, deep poverty, and sickness would soon be over for those who believe. At the meeting place, I noted how all females stayed on one side and all males stayed on the opposite side. The people observed this practice in accordance to the strong tradition they adhered to. I developed a severely hoarse voice from speaking at the top of my lungs through a small microphone just so the whole village would hear God's message. Blessed be Christ's name as thirty-six Hindus accepted the lavish gift of The Great Father and His Throne to the human race: Jesus Christ.

Thirty-six male and female followers came forward to renounce their old life of ignorance and made the solemn decision to surrender themselves to Jesus, the light of life as their new Protector, Lord, and Saviour. Surely the anthem of praise was played by the delighted angelic choir in heaven as they joyfully watched the awakened souls. One soul after another went down into the watery grave of Biblical Baptism officiated by an ever delighted pastor. I was so thrilled myself. I expressed my deep gratitude to the whole team , in my belief that "only God can repay them".

People jumped for joy when I handed out one hundred twenty Bibles, toothbrushes, and tubes of toothpaste as part of God's blessings that I was just glad to give as my humble Christmas gifts to them.

It was all worth it. It was worth crossing oceans and seas to soul-search for God's benighted children and to win them back to the loving Shepherd.

MY LORD AND I MINISTRY AND THE REDEEMING VOICE RADIO

Nothing is overdoing, nothing is going too far, and nothing is giving away too much when one beholds the great love and the great call to serve the Master for His glory. The heart of the willing and the submitted He will prune and utilize for the service.

After my return from India, I yearned to do more for the Lord. As I ventured on in faith, I launched two independent ministries: My Lord and I Ministry and The Redeeming Voice Radio. In my heart and in my mind there is not one that I know of who is literally everything in everything, under any and every circumstance, but the Lord Himself. So the ministry was born in total partnership with The Great Someone who offered a promise in the Book of Psalms 32:8:

> *"I will instruct you and teach you*
> *in the way you should go;*
> *I will guide you with My eye."*

The initiatives of both ministries aimed to reach far flung areas with the good news of salvation in Christ. I hoped to reach more people through printed pages and also through radio ministry. I earnestly sought for the Master Planner's direction and leadership as to where and through whom I could discover a way to impart light upon the Lamb of God who taketh away the sin of the world. I needed materials that would tremendously relate the melting love of God the Father and the overflowing pitying love of Christ to all souls. I made multiple phone calls asking where I could find inspired written materials that would somehow lead those who have been searching for God to alleviate them of their hopelessness, sorrow, sufferings, and pain. Many are longing for His divine presence in their lives so that they be restored physically, mentally, and spiritually. Maybe the printed materials that my heart was determined to find would lead them to Jesus of Nazareth, the answer to all our seeking and questioning.

I prayed for the Lord's intervention and lo and behold, the perfect hands of God paved the way to connect me with a couple by the names of Tim and Rose Schultz. They are humble and unassuming fieldworkers, both ever faithful and dedicated god-fearing servants. Their Literature Ministry demonstrates their full commitment as co-workers of Christ. This Literature Ministry is but one admirable story that I am so compelled to share for the glory of God. Over a span of nine years, a simple husband and wife have done their personal ministry by distributing over two million Gospel Tracts, Spirit of the Prophecy-filled literature to different parts of Canada through its postal unaddressed mailing program.

Tim is an American from California and Rose is a Canadian. Both in their mid-fifties, they hail from the countryside north of Toronto. They claim no material wealth of any kind nor do they hold any job to subsidize such an enormous service to the Lord. Their unwavering faith of total subsistence, the loving couple humbly profess, is driven by their implicit obedience to the divine instructions and direction of the Great Provider.

The godly written literatures are the Almighty Father's silent preachers in out-of-the-way places, smaller communities, and rural areas where the light has not yet been given and the seeds of truth still need to be sown.

A modest 275,000 copies were lowly pledged by My Lord and I Ministry, the majority of which were delivered to metro Toronto homes through unaddressed mailing. Some were shipped to different SDA churches in the Philippines for the multitude of souls hungering for the bread of life and thirsting for the water of life.

It is an inexplicable joy and gladness to recollect my mid-afternoon and early evening walks, not minding the heat or barking dogs, as I personally dropped off some of the Gospel-filled tabloids around the Mississauga area from one house mailbox to the next, onto parked cars along the streets, in churches, and in hospital, supermarket, and mall parking lots.

Under the umbrella of My Lord and I Ministry came the Redeeming Voice Radio Ministry that broadcast my seven-part series of "Jesus, My Lord Jesus is Everything" ("Jesus, ang Panginoon Kong si Jesus ay Lahat-lahat") from April 2015 to December 2015 on five radio stations in the Philippines. The series was also aired by Pan-American Broadcasting, a worldwide Christian Streaming Internet Radio Station, every four hours of the Sabbath during this period of time.

The Lord is instructing, He is guiding, and He is providing. More projects are unfolding, while others are in the making. My dear readers, I am sincerely soliciting your prayers on behalf of these endeavours, and for all others who are co-labouring together with the Returning Master, all in the sweetest and most awesome name of the begotten Son of God, Jesus Christ.

EPILOGUE

It was on the 30th of March, 2002 when I settled my heart and mind into the Way, the Truth, and the Life, Jesus, the Christ. I responded to the wooing of the Holy Spirit and was divinely compelled to publicly profess my submission of faith to the Son of God, as my Lord and Saviour, through baptism. In spirit and in truth I went down into the watery grave renouncing my old life of sin, and out of the water, I came to be a newborn Christian and a child of God - an event in my life that is recorded in the book of heaven as well.

My love for the Father and His Son Jesus Christ is distinctly incomparable to any relationships on earth, a heaven and earth difference from the romantic love that Matt and I had during our whirlwind courtship. It is a love that is exceedingly contradictory to the love that I swore to give during my marriage oath.

But the precious love of Jesus is something that is wonderful and beyond description. I can only respond in awe and in reverence to the new values and aspirations that my Lord gives. Who am I not to respond with an irreversible new commitment to Him?

As a new Christian, I take pride in being a member of the humble movement of the risen Saviour, a movement He commissioned to continue what the Father and Son started so that no one will perish but be ready to stand before the solemn day of accounting that is drawing near. God's called out people, who rose prophetically, are the recipient and executor of God's final assignment to warn the world of Christ's imminent return.

This movement of the faithful and called, who remain loyal, has been guided, guarded, and divinely directed by the hands and eyes of the great "I am", "the Ancient of Days", the undisputed ancestry of which is well documented in the Holy Scriptures, beginning from Genesis and up to the last book of Revelation.

From the lips of the world's greatest Missionary who said, "come and follow Me", "Go", "teach", "baptize", that the movement crossed great oceans and mighty seas, rugged mountains and dark prison cells, for the love of God to be advertised, and that there is a new earth that is coming not too long from now.

Let the sweet name of Jesus be heard from the farthest of the east to the west, from the north to the south of the habitable globe, that those, who have never heard about Jesus, will hear about Him. That those, who have not known Jesus, will come to know Him. That those, who have never met Jesus, will come to meet Jesus.

What a privilege indeed to be called to spread the three angels' message of Revelation 14:6-9 - the pressing messages of an appeal which is at the same time a great warning to the entire planet, so that no one should tarry nor take it for granted.

I gladly embraced the Bible-based fundamental teachings of my spiritual family on earth. I wish I could share with you the full in-depth exposition, but my limited skills could only submit to the seasoned Bible scholars whom I believe exercised their faithfulness to the Word of God.

What a prerogative indeed to be connected with a lineage that has not deviated from the sure way. What a privilege it is to pass on the blazing torch of truth no matter how, no matter what, not because they have to, but because they want to, because of the love of the "Sovereign of the Universe" God, the Father, and His only begotten Son, Jesus Christ, in whom all came and by whom all was begun.

AFTERTHOUGHT

I am reluctant to end my life's story for the simple reason that the cries of my heart for innumerable long nights of countless years that my loved ones will come to faith in Christ still await realization. But the reality remains that no matter how many long miles I have run, if I do not acknowledge my insufficiency and dependence on His all-sufficiency, then my situation of spiritual battle is humanly impossible. What Jesus said in John 15:5 is as clear as the sunshine: "for without me you can do nothing." He demands not a half but a full, a completely surrendered heart and mind.

God knows the very thoughts in my head and the intentions of my heart. Even the fall of a sparrow on the ground does not go unnoticed in the eyes of God, so how much more does he see us whom He created in His own likeness. He knew me perfectly before I was knitted in my mother's womb and He knows that as I came to exist in this fallen earth, without His Son Christ Jesus I am capable of no good, with my walk in life only tantamount to an undeniable truth, being aimless, meaningless, and worthless in tread and stride.

My God has been trimming my lamp. My need of oil He replenishes time and again. In my pleading and asking for His help He brought me to the end of my strength so that I will trust in His ability to do the impossible for me. He wants me to acknowledge that it must be Him who takes the full control of the steering wheel, otherwise I will short-circuit His power. He has bid every child of His to "Be still and know that I am God" (Psalm 46:10).

It is only in Jesus, by Jesus, and through the promptings of the Holy Spirit of God that I can learn to master His dos and don'ts to obedience and learn to subdue and overcome the artful tactics and sophisticated and cunning ways of the determined enemy in my unguarded moments. He taught me to bite my lips when my tongue is about to deliver aggression and judgmental criticisms that make the Father frown.

My ever suffering God has helped me by educating and renewing my erratic life. Likewise, my God is patient with my husband, as he reluctantly learns to acknowledge his own futile manners and allows God to perfect His work in His own good time.

I mused at the transformation that was unfolding in me. I have praised and thanked the Lord and decided to let Him do the work. I anticipate bright things to come, when my man Tom Brozo will unveil the person that he was when I first met him: so confident and full of hope. I am now imagining seeing my man's personality shine as he regains the gentleman that is in him. I have always believed that Tom can be that same person who captured my youthful admirations, if he would put his mind to it. I will support and encourage him to regain that respectability and honour that God has in store for him.

There is nothing impossible with God. I have faith and confidence in His words through the Prophet Jeremiah: "Behold, I am the Lord, the God of all flesh, is there anything too hard for Me?" (Jeremiah 32:27). How could anything be too difficult for the Lord who spoke the universe into existence? I cannot promise nor boast of my tomorrow, for I know not what tomorrow will bring (Prov.27:1).

The exercise of willpower is better than making rosy promises. I choose to remain a wife to Tom. Yes, I choose to be forgiving since I have experienced the joy of being forgiven by my God and the contentment of dwelling in freedom from guilt and shame. Zechariah the Prophet wrote, "Not by might nor by power, but by my Spirit says the Lord of hosts" (Zechariah 4:6).

It would be wonderful for both Tom and I to rediscover love and to transcend yet a higher level of marriage fulfillment, even in the autumn of our lives, when both of us could together say, "See what God has wrought."

Bible texts are from The New King James Version (NKJV) unless noted otherwise.

Seventh-day Adventists Beliefs, Pacific Press Publishing Association, Boise, ID 83653.

Seventh-day Adventist Hymnal, Review and Herald Publishing Association, Washington, DC 20039-0555; Hagerstown, MD 21740.

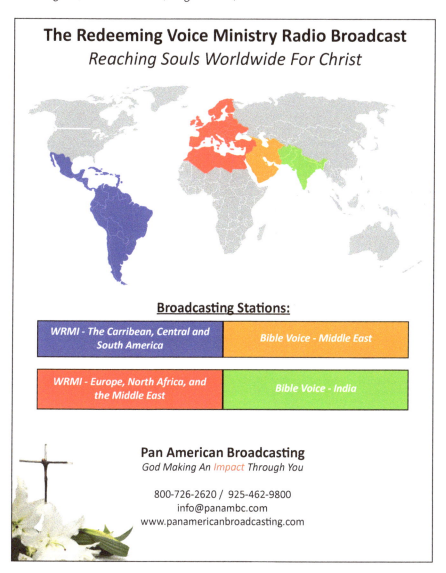

Nora Ruiz Ednacot Brozo

PAN AMERICAN BROADCASTING

GOD MAKING AN IMPACT THROUGH YOU

7011 Koll Center Parkway, Suite 250
Pleasanton CA 94566-3253
Toll Free: 800-726-2620
Main Office: 925-462-9800
Fax: 925-462-9808

www.panamericanbroadcasting.com

December 15, 2016

Sis. Nora Brozo
My Lord And I Ministry
208-3575 Kaneff Cresent
Mississauga, ON L5R 3Y5

Blessings to you Sis. Brozo,

For over 80 years Pan American Broadcasting has been assisting ministries with Global Outreach opportunities through radio, television, and internet broadcasting, providing unique, affordable, and dynamic opportunities for ministries in the US and around the world. Our platforms can reach millions of listeners at once, providing the much needed support of the Word of God in urban and rural areas of the world...Amen!

What a blessing it is to announce that *The Redeeming Voice Ministry* will begin broadcasting January 7th, 2017 via Pan American Broadcasting's partnering Outreach services – "Bible Voice Middle East", "Bible Voice India", "WRMI South America", and "WRMI Europe, Middle East, and North Africa". Your broadcast will be heard throughout the Indian Subcontinent, the Middle East, Europe, North Africa, the Caribbean, and Central and South America, broadcasting on dynamic and powerful shortwave signals as follows:

Bible Voice India – This 100,000 watt shortwave station broadcasts into Pakistan, Afghanistan, Nepal, India, and Bangladesh reaching a potential audience of approximately 1.4 billion souls! Your program will be heard every Saturday 1545 UTC (9:45 PM local time in India).

Bible Voice Middle East – This 100,000 watt shortwave station reaches Syria, Lebanon, Israel, Gaza, Jordan, Northern Egypt, Turkey, Armenia, Yemen, Oman, and Saudi Arabia with a potential audience reach of over 288 million souls! Your program will be heard every Saturday 1715 UTC (8:15 PM local time in Israel).

WRMI South America – This 100,000 watt shortwave station reaches the Caribbean, Central America, and South America, with a potential audience reach of over 623 million souls! Your program will be heard every Saturday at 0200 UTC.

WRMI Europe, Middle East, and North Africa – This 100,000 watt shortwave station reaches countries including England, France, Germany, Italy, Spain, Bulgaria, Turkey, Greece, Syria, Lebanon, Israel, Iraq, Saudi Arabia, Egypt, Libya, Tunisia, Algeria, and Morocco, with a potential outreach of over 1.15 billion souls. Your program will be heard every Saturday at 2030 UTC.

From all of us at Pan American Broadcasting we are excited to welcome you back to our family of broadcasters. We continue to pray for you and your radio outreach, and we have faith that your messages and teachings will be a blessing to your listening audiences. Should you have any questions regarding your broadcast, please contact us at 800-726-2620 or 925-462-9500.

God Bless

Jeff Bernald & the Pan American Broadcasting Team

Reaching Behind Bars

Sis. Nora Brozo of "My Lord & I Ministry" shares hope through her inspirational message for the prison inmates during one of the visits of the team.

Since 2012, two groups of volunteers ministering in two prison sites are bringing hope to the hopeless locked behind the bars of the Bulihan (Silang, Cavite) Municipal Jail (BMJ) and the GMA Municipal Jail (GMAMJ). Grounded on the Biblical principle of Matthew 25:36, the Behind Bars Ministry of the local church has been bringing messages of hope through once-a-week visits to these jails. However, the sincere service of the volunteers was constrained by the limitation of fund. It was God's purpose that it will not remain this way, miles away from these places the Lord touched the heart of unfamiliar lady generously offering what she have bringing hope to the inmates.

In early 2015, My Lord & I Ministry supported the endeavours in these two prison sites. The Ministry funded the provision of Bibles to prison inmates, guitars which are used during song services, and printed uniform-shirts for volunteers. To date, 152 Bibles have been distributed to inmates in BJMP & GMAMP. Two guitars, one for each site, songbooks, once a month meals for 496 inmates were also provided and printed uniforms for volunteers were distributed.

My Lord and I Ministry works hand in hand with the local Seventh-day Adventist Church in Maderan, G.M.A. Cavite, Philippines to grasp the unreached and the indigent. The Ministry has been supporting the local church's outreach endeavours that aim to introduce the love of the Father through acts of kindness and the hope of salvation through Christ Jesus.

CPSIA information can be obtained
at www.ICGtesting.com
Printed in the USA
BVHW060717280420
578269BV00004B/87